D0351596

WOMEN
at work

WOMEN
at work

Strategies for
SURVIVAL and **SUCCESS**

Anne Dickson

KOGAN
PAGE

First published in 2000
Reprinted 2001

Apart from any fair dealing for the purposes of research or private study, or criticism or review, as permitted under the Copyright, Designs and Patents Act 1988, this publication may only be reproduced, stored or transmitted, in any form or by any means, with the prior permission in writing of the publishers, or in the case of reprographic reproduction in accordance with the terms and licences issued by the CLA. Enquiries concerning reproduction outside these terms should be sent to the publishers at the undermentioned addresses:

Kogan Page Limited
120 Pentonville Road
London
N1 9JN
UK

Kogan Page Limited
163 Central Avenue, Suite 2
Dover
NH 03820
USA

© Anne Dickson, 2000

The right of Anne Dickson to be identified as the author of this work has been asserted by her in accordance with the Copyright, Designs and Patents Act 1988.

British Library Cataloguing in Publication Data

A CIP record for this book is available from the British Library.

ISBN 0 7494 3373 6

Typeset by Jean Cussons Typesetting, Diss, Norfolk
Printed and bound in Great Britain by Clays Ltd, St Ives plc

Contents

Acknowledgements

The inspiration for this book was generated by the courage, daring, humour and vulnerability of the women who have trusted and worked with me over the years.

The energy to commit my ideas to paper was provided by a thunderbolt of anger, prompted by a conversation over lunch with Frances Kelly, who explained with exquisite clarity the limitations of the publishing scene in the UK after a decade under American parent companies.

A congenial space in which to write was offered by friends: Paola and Alex very kindly made part of their home available to me for several weeks last year, when the atmosphere around my own home made it impossible to write.

Practical help came at various stages: Karola McCormack typed the early drafts of the manuscript; the initial editing was done by Liz Clasen, whose generosity and support have become such an essential part of my writing that I may be in danger of taking her for granted; Beverley Baillie kindly prepared the diagrams for the text; Jenny Russell prepared the final manuscript for the publishers, her insights and enthusiasm transforming our work from a tedious chore into something approaching fun.

Finally, I would like to acknowledge Richard Boot at the University of Lancaster, who brings a poetic soul to his teaching and writing about management and organizational development. I am grateful for his ideas and his vision.

Introduction – the gap between competence and confidence

I first thought about writing this book two years ago while travelling home after running a Personal Development course for women staff. As usual, I was ruminating on the events, exchanges and excitement of our time working together. It was hard work for us all and I was, as ever, moved by the courage of the participants, their cooperation and general openness to change.

On this particular journey I found myself pondering on an extraordinary paradox I had witnessed many times whenever I have worked with women in management positions. This paradox can be found in academic, health, educational or commercial settings in England, Scandinavia, Eastern Europe or Japan. On one hand is the high level of academic or professional qualification and experience of these women, their intelligence, their talents, their commitment and dedication; while on the other is a vivid picture of internal doubts, misgivings and anxieties stemming from an abiding, and sometimes disabling, *lack of confidence.*

Sometimes this relates to specific situations, but often it is a more generalized lack of confidence that permeates every interaction.

This book explores and explains the paradox – looking at the experience of individual women in the workplace, the problems they encounter and why. It then addresses the situation with practical skills and suggestions as to how to develop a genuine belief in your own ability to communicate, to be effective, to manage your authority and weather the storms of working life with more confidence.

The content of the book is based on the content of the courses I have taught for many years. Why do women attend? What do they hope to learn? Below are samples of their own words:

I'd like to be able to...

Make articulate contributions at/in meetings where I am the junior but by no means the least intelligent participant.

Handle conflict and negotiation constructively.

Cope better with 'macho' culture and norms.

Say 'No' in a positive manner.

Feel more comfortable receiving criticism.

Have my views heard without appearing insensitive or aggressive.

Be recognized as an important member of staff.

Assert more authority with my staff without being authoritarian/bossy.

Stand up for myself with male managers.

Feel more confidence in handling interpersonal conflict.

Know how to cope better with the fact that I am quite honest and forthright in my opinions, which some people find difficult.

Show that it is possible to commit to your job as well as having a personal life: to be accepted on an equal footing with career men who have children.

Deal with difficult people: by difficult I mean people who are not willing to listen and those who do not value my opinions.

Gain a better sense of my own strengths and values.

Stop being over-compliant and agreeing to help others because this leads to my not meeting my own targets.

Ensure that my voice is heard when I make requests.

Look at how one places value on oneself and one's own needs.

Strike a better balance: if I'm assertive, people say I'm aggressive, but when I'm not assertive people walk all over me.

Stand my ground even when I am being stereotyped.

Come out of the course with greater self-confidence about my own wishes and goals.

Deal with senior figures who don't take me seriously.

Handle conflict better because it causes me enormous personal stress at the moment. I also end up blaming myself even though I can see I am not in the wrong.

Feel more confidence: after taking maternity leave I feel the need to re-assert myself.

Deal with male aggression without becoming upset.

Deal with colleagues and difficult issues in a climate of constant change and pressure.

Be effective at chairing meetings and confronting people who will not keep to the point.

Deal with male colleagues so that I am not stereotyped as an overbearing woman.

Speak up if I have something to say without being talked out of it.

Deal constructively with more senior staff who always give negative criticism, never praise.

Exercise authority and power without losing my ground.

Manage better the conflict between personal values and those of the organization.

Learn skills I can use when under pressure to take on work that I don't have time to do and that I know will be detrimental to my output.

Deal with male colleagues who are not pulling their weight without being labelled a 'nag'.

Gain increased confidence in my own opinion and to learn about voice production: can a softer voice be assertive?

Act on and express disagreement and anger especially with senior male colleagues.

Voice my own needs and objectives and put them into practice.

Confront workplace bullying and prejudice.

Interrupt my manager going on and on, without appearing rude.

Learn ways of boosting my self-confidence and self-esteem.

Gain practical skills in expressing my needs, eg access to equipment and technical assistance because at the moment my work suffers and I don't achieve as much as others.

Find some support because I feel that there is less and less of this at present.

Several themes recur:

- speaking up clearly and communicating needs and objectives;
- saying 'No' positively;

- managing anger/stress/being 'upset';
- managing criticism and put-downs;
- handling conflict;
- managing personal authority more effectively;
- handling the clash between personal values and those of the organization;
- gender issues at work.

The common denominator in all these themes is lack of confidence. The meaning of confidence here is not based on any idealized sense of ever-present competence. It does not rely on coercion, on being right, on winning, on being impervious to the ordinary fluctuations of human life and hormones.

The confidence we are seeking to develop and build is based on being true to oneself, on managing anxiety and other feelings instead of being paralysed or overwhelmed by them, and learning communication skills that *work* even in difficult situations.

one

Assertive – substance or stereotype?

Often I start a course by looking at current assertive stereo-types because women arrive with a certain model of assertiveness in mind and a certain brand of confidence in mind, especially if they have attended previous courses in assertiveness training.

It is important to introduce my working model because this will underpin every interaction, every role-play, and will shape my teaching and the learning of the entire course.

To understand the current stereotype of assertive behaviour, we have to go back to look at the history of this subject in this country. Twenty-two years ago, I taught the first evening class in assertiveness. The relevance of the subject to women's lives and their consequent interest in learning the skills were immediately evident. Participants learnt a new concept of empowerment: one that embraced the importance of communicating feelings and the concept of equality with others.

Throughout the 10 weeks, women would learn to be less mistrustful of other women, therefore less competitive, and more supportive as they identified with other women's experience, even if that experience was different from their own. They learnt to challenge, confront and correct each other (and myself), and to develop a true confidence. This class collaboration would often result in a peer group meeting after the official class had finished, continuing to practise role-play together sometimes for a year or so after.

As the demand for classes grew I established a national and

later international training association which offered a 12-month, in-depth training in assertiveness and sexuality work for women who wanted to teach these skills within their own personal and work contexts.

In 1982, my book, *A Woman in Your Own Right*, was published. By now I had modified the material, derived from the work of American behavioural psychologists, so that it reflected my own emphasis on the responsible expression of emotion, the relevance of assertive skills to sexuality and my commitment to equality.

In the mid-1980s, assertiveness training became trendy and the resulting bandwagon attracted hundreds of people to set themselves up as teachers and trainers, often with little or no experience. Over the long term, it became diluted as a subject, as the more radical elements were filtered out. Only the easier and more acceptable aspects were taught, which meant that management of emotions, especially anger, handling criticism, sexuality and the importance of equality were frequently omitted.

Assertiveness was further diluted because role-play was either not used at all, or used inappropriately. This meant that participants would learn the concepts intellectually but without the crucial opportunity to practise these skills within a safe setting and then be able to transfer them to real life.

A third influence was operative at this time. In the early days women were able to identify strongly with the disadvantages of not being able to speak up or set limits with the current awareness of inequalities with men in their personal and working lives. Men on the whole were not interested. An unassertive person was passive, weak, shy and unable to give orders: an ineffectual image that most men were able to dismiss as irrelevant to themselves. Over time, however, men began to realize that there was more to assertiveness than they had thought.

As this shift was occurring, assertiveness was taken up by the commercial sector. The early grass roots image changed into a big business image, taught within organizations, usually for men and women together. The going was hard sometimes, I remember, knowing that a breakthrough in understanding and practice that occurred for individuals during a course was quite different from challenging the prevailing ethos of competition, dominance and hierarchy within the organization as a whole.

The general financial climate towards the end of that decade meant that specialists like myself were no longer viable. Those in charge of training departments economized by offering a training package themselves. Such a package typically included stress reduction, time management, team building and confrontation skills: assertiveness simply became part of the package. People did the best they could but the core elements of assertiveness training were even further reduced, and the practice of role-play disappeared completely.

The combination of all these influences has led to the current anomaly whereby the concepts of assertiveness training are familiar to a large part of the population and the word assertive is common parlance, and at the same time, the concepts and the word are usually misrepresented.

This explains why participants arrive in confusion: When does authoritative become authoritarian? How can one be the boss without being bossy? How do we handle the power that is part of our working responsibility without being oppressive? When is behaviour aggressive and when is it assertive?

The boundary lines have been blurred over and over again; it is not surprising that the meaning is unclear when the reference point is itself out of alignment. When the model is unclear, any attempts to assess or evaluate our behaviour, any effort we may make to be assertive in our interaction with others, will also be out of alignment and ultimately leave us confused and... *unconfident.*

This has meant that many women have experienced assertiveness training in some form but often with only a superficial benefit. The practical consequences are seen in organizations. There are many more women managers than there were 10 years ago but women in senior positions still remain rare. Despite the optimism and money behind the government-funded 'Opportunity 2000' campaign, the promoters acknowledge that the aim was not achieved. Women who are either middle or senior managers do not operate from a core of high self-esteem: privately they often feel lonely, unconfident and are working excessively hard to compensate for self-perceived inadequacy.

So now we have a situation where everyone refers to assertiveness training as if we were referring to the same thing: the reality is that we are not. I want to focus on some of these underlying popular assumptions. They are so deep and powerful that, currently, the prevailing stereotype of assertive behaviour could be more accurately described as 'aggression in velvet gloves'. Outright hostility and overt aggression are less acceptable but now we have a more insidious model: the assertive person, according to stereotype, is confident, articulate, prepared, unfazed, invulnerable and effective – in short, always and in every way, a *winner*. The goal is generally understood to be achieved by learning mechanical techniques, with an appropriate script and delivery. This generates associations of cloning, which is why many people are put off by the concept of assertiveness.

There is no room in this model for being vulnerable, caught on the hop, being confused, mistaken or uncertain, in other words, for being human. Many women say to themselves: 'When I am confident and calm and clear and articulate, *then* I'll speak up.' So they wait and wait and wait. Instead of being seen as a normal indication of the difficulty of the task ahead, anxiety is interpreted as weakness, as a sign of inadequacy. In fact, anxiety can be managed very effectively through proper learning and practice of assertive skills.

A second assumption spawned by the above model is that certain individuals are either aggressive or assertive or passive all the time. This is not true. We are all capable of behaving in all these ways at different times, with different people, in different situations. Whenever we feel at a disadvantage, we resort to any familiar tactics we have available as a form of defence. When we stop feeling defensive, we have a lot more choice.

The assumptions that guilt or anxiety must be denied, and that one must conform to a stereotype of how one *should* be, are both counterproductive. Learning to be more fully oneself is the base of personal power. This is the pivot of my teaching and will be explored and explained in the following chapters.

Being assertive, I believe, springs from a fulcrum of equality. It springs from balance between self and others, from being human, being less restrained by doubt and insecurity so that you can become more fully true to yourself in every way.

two

Speaking up

A lot of our communication happens so automatically that we don't have time to really notice what occurs. We assume another person will respond aggressively without realizing that, often, we elicit that very reaction through our tone of voice or choice of words. We fret about being ignored or dismissed, while unconsciously giving the other person a clear impression that what we want to say is not worth listening to anyway.

The following list will give an idea of common difficulties experienced at work:

Handling interruptions

Communicating needs and objectives

Handling the clash between personal values and those of the organization

Managing personal authority more effectively

Speaking up in meetings

Managing stress/anger/being 'upset'

Holding one's ground

Saying 'No' positively

Handling conflict

Asking for an improvement in somebody's work

Managing others' aggression

I have already written specifically about assertive techniques in my book *A Woman in Your Own Right* so here I will only revise them.

We have to focus on the actual components of our interaction with others in real-life situations to understand what happens. The most basic and a difficult skill to learn is *being specific*. Women experience this difficulty in personal, social and work situations and it can be traced at root to a fundamental confusion about how we define ourselves. Through the habit of a lifetime and aeons of conditioning, we often lose our own personal reference point in our efforts to please, placate, conform to, rebel against, avoid, punish or control *others*. Consequently, a common starting point of our communication is the OTHER:

'If he's aggressive...

'If she's nice...

'Because he's the boss...

'If she's uncooperative...

'As he's an idiot...

'As I know she's going to be difficult...

... I will adjust my behaviour accordingly.'

We imagine, we predict, we play out the scenario in our minds, we assume we know the outcome before we start. Our anticipation of the other person's response increases our anxiety and becomes a conviction. Through the distorted perception of the high levels of anxiety, we decide there's no point and so give up or else we go in with all guns blazing.

It is easy to become so preoccupied with the other person's real or imagined responses, and our responses in imagined reply, that we completely lose sight of what we want and what we want to say. We have to learn to locate the starting point in any interaction in *ourselves*: What do *I* want? What do *I* feel? At this stage, it doesn't matter whether or not you are going to get it: what you need to know is specifically what you want.

Carol, a research officer, wanted to ask the secretarial assistant to do some typing. My first question to Carol was, 'What do you want?' Carol's first reply was, 'She is always a bit dismissive.'

And so our dialogue continued:

AD: 'What do you want to ask?'
Carol: 'She is working for three other people, not just me.'
AD: What do you want to ask?'
Carol: 'She always puts other people's work as a priority and leaves mine till last.'
AD: 'What do you want to ask her to do?'
Carol: 'I'd like her to do some typing.'
AD: 'What do you want her to type?'
Carol: 'A report.'
AD: 'When do you want it by?'
Carol   *(shrug of shoulders)*: 'Tuesday?'
AD: 'Is that what you want?'
Carol: 'Well, that will do.'
AD: 'When would you like it?'
Carol: 'Well... by the last post.'
AD: 'So when do you need it by to get the last post?'
Carol: 'It leaves at five so I would have to have it by three.'
AD: 'So your request is "I'd like you to type this report by 3 o'clock so that I will have time to check it by the last post"?'
Carol: 'Yes.'
BINGO!

This filtering of our thought processes happens every time. Carol is intelligent, articulate and competent: what stops her being specific is the ingrained habit of using the *other person* as the automatic starting point and the consequent spiral of anxiety.

With help and discipline, you can work out, in excruciatingly specific detail, exactly what it is you want. This is the starting point. Next we look at how we can communicate this request even when we are feeling anxious.

Role-play practice involves Carol being herself. This is inevitably difficult because we are all used to maintaining an image of absolute competence, especially at work. What prevents any of us from behaving assertively is not the experience of anxiety in itself, but our inability to *manage* that anxiety. Like any other feeling, anxiety is a psychosomatic experience; in other words, it occurs simultaneously *in the mind and the body*. The correct use of role-play allows a participant to manage anxiety as she experiences it: psychosomatically. Without role-play, a participant will only learn at a cognitive level. This can be stimulating but is unlikely to lead to lasting behaviour change in the real-life situation.

The context for role-play needs to be utterly safe and supportive for it to work. Fear – of judgement, looking foolish, being criticized for making mistakes – is ever present, so safety within the group is essential for anyone to take the risk of being real instead of play-acting.

Practice 1

On her first attempt, Carol's interaction went something like this:

She walks through the door of the assistant's office.

Carol: 'Hi, I wondered whether it would be possible for you to type this by 3 o'clock. Please do you think you could manage it for me?'

Assistant: 'I suppose so.'

Carol's learning 1

Instead of questions, use statements. This doesn't mean never asking a question, but our chronic tendency to make requests in the form of questions actually undermines our authority:

'Would you mind doing this again for me?'

'Could you just be a dear and phone X?'

'Would you do me a big favour and...?'

These questions are usually asked in a tone ranging from sweet to whining and the intention behind them is:

- not to offend;
- not to appear bossy;
- not to be rude;
- not to be seen as aggressive.

Unfortunately the effect on the other person is at best wishy-washy and at worst manipulative.

Practice 2

Carol walks through the door.

Carol (a bit brusquely): 'Hi, I wondered whether... I mean, I would like you to type this by 3 o'clock this afternoon, okay?'
Assistant (a little surprised): 'Okay.'

In the feedback, the 'assistant' said that Carol had been clearer but a bit abrupt.

Carol's learning 2

As often happens when we try to eliminate the sweet talk, we tend to be a little curt and aggressive. Consider the other person as a human being. Who is this person? Is she a nameless secretarial assistant or flesh and blood too? As Carol describes Jackie, it emerges that Jackie's office houses the coffee machine so that she is constantly being interrupted, so no wonder she is often short-tempered with people.

Making the interaction more equal is allowing yourself to see the person at the other end of the request. You can only do this comfortably *after* you have sorted out what you want. If you start by thinking of the other person's concerns like Carol did at the beginning, you will never get going. So once you know (from your own reference point) where you start, you can afford to consider the other person from a more mutual point of respect.

Practice 3

Carol walks through the door.

Carol: 'Hi, Jackie. This report is really urgent and I would like it ready by 3 o'clock so that I can check it before getting the last post. Is that going to be possible?'
Jackie: 'Yes, I don't see any problem.'
Carol: 'Thanks a lot. See you later.'

She leaves Jackie's office.

Carol's learning 3

By adding to her request that the report is urgently needed, which it is, Carol is making a stronger statement for herself. Addressing Jackie by name at the beginning and thanking her as she leaves helps to acknowledge Jackie's contribution as an equal. These two points were endorsed by the person taking the part of Jackie in the role-play. She said that, in the final practice, she experienced Carol's approach as certain and clear, and she found herself taking the request more seriously.

Speaking up at a meeting presents a different challenge.

Sue, a nurse tutor, found herself intimidated in meetings where she was in the minority of one or two women with a majority of male staff.

Practice 1

Discussion in progress.

Sue's first attempt left her sitting anxiously looking at others, unable to find any words and waiting for the moment to speak.

Sue's learning 1

There is no right moment so don't bother to wait for it. The longer you wait, the more anxious you become, and this process escalates, making it physically harder to speak up. Then the moment has gone, the topic of discussion changes and once again, you are left feeling cheated, resentful or cross with yourself.

The only thing to do is breathe deeply and take the plunge. It helps to address someone by name. If you can't, try a simple phrase:

'I'd like to speak...'

'I'd like to make a suggestion...'

'I'd like to disagree...'

'I'd like to say something...'

Nothing will make it easy. It is no use waiting for a benign chairperson to notice that you want to speak and invite you to do so, assuring you that your comments will be valued. You can dream on, or go for it.

Practice 2

Discussion in progress.

Sue (*supported, encouraged, anxious, her heart thumping*) opens her mouth and says: 'I'd like to say something.'
  The discussion stops and everyone looks at her.
  Sue in turn looks at me and asks, 'Now what do I do?'

Sue's learning 2

It is difficult to speak up in the first place but once you have the attention, you face a second wave of anxiety. All you can do is to keep practising.

Practice 3

Discussion in progress.

Sue (a little bolder this time): 'Excuse me, I'd like to say something. Wouldn't it be better if we looked more closely at the needs of the students?'

Sue's learning 3

Sue discovers that her fear is based on the past experience of being ignored when she has actually ventured to express an opinion. So we add another strategy here which helps to manage the situation. Once you have made your suggestion, open out the discussion and *invite* a response specifically. This helps take the spotlight away from yourself and also helps to encourage others to contribute in response to your suggestion. In this way, if others agree with you, there will be more chance of their opinions being heard, as well.

Practice 4

Discussion in progress.

Sue (bolder still): 'Excuse me, I'd like to say something. I'd prefer to look more closely at the actual needs of the students than talking theoretically.'
   (Letting her eyes pass around some of the group members): 'I'd like to know how others of you feel about this.'

Sue's learning 4

With practice you can still be anxious and open your mouth at the same time. Even if your heart is thumping you can ride out the anxiety without being overwhelmed by it.

   As a general rule, others are unlikely to be as aware of your nervousness as you are yourself. This is why it's important to keep going. Each time that you do, your confidence is reinforced.

Making eye contact

Over and over again, I find in classes that women do not consciously realize that while they are speaking, their eyes are focused on the floor or into the middle distance, slightly above people's heads.

   It makes a huge difference to the effect you create when you make eye contact. The reason we look away is simply a by-product of anxiety: it is a submissive response, to ward off aggression. The only way to address this is to consciously make yourself look around at others. Make yourself glance directly into the eyes of your listeners, randomly going around the group. You have to make yourself physically turn your head and neck to the left and to the right, quite mechanically at first. If you are not used to doing this, it feels wooden, strange and unnatural to begin with, but with practice and repetition, it soon becomes easier and more automatic.

The good news is that, as many course members discover from their fellow participants, it doesn't actually look as strange as it feels. You may feel like a robot but it doesn't come across. What does come across is a more direct and effective style of delivery. This means that others are more drawn to pay attention and to respond because you are communicating with more conviction. This is why it is worth making the effort – as one of the steps towards taking yourself more seriously.

three

Taking yourself seriously

One of the most frequent complaints I hear from women at work is: 'They don't take me seriously.'

While this may or may not be true, what we look at next is the way in which we fail to take *ourselves* seriously with the result that, often, our complaint about someone else's lack of respect or attention is a direct consequence of our own way of communicating.

The first step in taking yourself seriously is to consider what it is you really want, as we have looked at already. Now consider how you are going to present this.

Jane, a lecturer, wanted to tackle her boss about the lack of support and contact with him during the six months she had been in her post in this particular department.

In the same way as before, we worked together to filter out a variety of anticipated responses and her anxieties:

'He's always too busy.'

'He's friendly but just won't listen.'

'He'll think I'm inadequate.'

'If I say something, I'll look stupid.'

Eventually, she was clear she wanted to ask specifically for a discussion about her work in the department.

Practice 1

She set up her role-play as she imagined handling the interaction. She anticipated bumping into her boss in the corridor on his way to a meeting, which is how she'd always attempted to make contact with him in the past.

Jane: 'Excuse me, do you have a minute? I wondered if I could have a word with you about my work sometime...?'

Jane's learning 1

In order to talk about something that is important to you, you have to *set the scene*. Setting the scene is a vital strategy that helps to manage our anxiety. It is anxiety that makes us blurt things out, interrupt others, try to get someone's attention while they are on their way to somewhere else. It is anxiety that makes our tone of voice uncertain and our words trail into silence. It is our own anxiety that prevents us from expressing exactly how important something is to us.

Jane learnt that an alternative was to phone/visit her boss *in advance*.

Practice 2

Jane: 'Do you have a minute?'
Boss: 'Just about.'
Jane: 'I would like to talk with you about my work. Could we arrange to meet for 10 minutes, if you can fit it in?'
Boss: 'Is it important?'
Jane: 'Yes, it is... quite.'
Boss (*as he leaves the office*): 'Well, we'll manage it sometime next week, okay?'

Jane's learning 2

If what you want to say is important to you, say so. Jane asked for 10 minutes. When I challenged her about this, she realized it wasn't long enough. She expanded her request to half an hour. When challenged again she realized that, as it was important and would affect the whole of her future work, she really needed an hour: to talk about her experience, to ask questions, to have a full discussion of how to implement future changes.

So the first way that Jane failed to take herself seriously was by being too casual; the second way was by undercutting the time necessary for such an important discussion; the third way was by failing to state how important this meeting was to her.

Practice 3

Jane enters the office.

Jane: 'Hello, do you have a minute?'
Boss: 'Just about.'
Jane: 'I would like to talk to you about something impor-tant. I would like to arrange an hour. When would be convenient?'
Boss: 'An *hour*?! What on earth is it about?'
Jane: 'It's about the six months I have been in this depart-ment. I would like to discuss it all with you.'
Boss: 'What is there to talk about? You are doing fine, aren't you?'
Jane: 'Well, sort of... but I'd like to talk to you.'
Boss: 'Can't you tell me what it's about? I've got 10 minutes now.'

Jane hesitates.

Jane's learning 3

It's hard to hold your ground. Jane worries – like we often do – that she hasn't really got the right to ask for time, hasn't really got the right to ask for a whole hour, and when her boss protests, finds herself wondering if she could really manage on her own after all. Maybe she has got it all out of proportion. Maybe she is *imagining* that she needs to talk it through. And so on.

It is crucial not to be drawn into talking there and then, on the spot, when you are not prepared and, equally importantly, when the boss has his mind on countless other things.

Taking yourself seriously doesn't mean overriding others' needs or priorities. This is often a concern here: do I have the right to ask for somebody else's time? Answer: yes. This is where we have to return to the core of assertiveness as equality. He is the boss: he is higher than you in the hierarchy, he may be older or more qualified, or more knowledgeable, and he *may* be busier.

However, Jane is also working hard. She is busy. Why does she want to talk things through? Why is it important to her? Because she cannot do her work effectively otherwise. Not because she wants to waste his time, not because she has nothing better to do, not because she is inadequate or incompetent. She wants to see him because the past six months have been disorganized and unclear with a lot of wasted time and effort on her part, and much of this is because her boss did not attend to his responsibilities in regard to her in the first place.

Seeing that her reason for asking is actually to the benefit of the whole organization gives Jane some confidence with which to balance her misgivings and self-doubt.

Practice 4

Jane enters the office.

Jane:	'Tim, I would like to arrange a time to talk to you. We will need an hour. When can you manage this?'
Tim:	'An hour?! What on earth for?'
Jane:	'I know you are busy, but this discussion is important to me. It's important to both of us in fact. I would like to arrange an hour when it is convenient.'
Tim:	'Well I don't know. Can't you tell me what it's about?'
Jane:	'It may sound silly but I'd prefer not to start talking about it now. It is important but it will wait until we meet. When do you have an hour free?'
Tim:	'Maybe next week sometime.'
Jane:	'Which day next week would suit you? Tuesday or Wednesday would be good for me.'
Tim:	'Okay then, Tuesday at four.'
Jane:	'Thanks. I'll see you then.' (Leaves Tim's office.)

Jane's learning 4

Once again, the feedback from the person taking Tim's role reinforced Jane's change in attitude: her tone of voice and posture were less apologetic and she conveyed that the matter was important and that her request had to be considered seriously.

Another way in which we often undermine ourselves is by speaking to somebody before getting their attention. Beryl found it very hard to make a simple request of a computer technician colleague. She managed to make her request, she told us, but complained that he never took any notice and persistently failed to give her the information to which he had easy access.

Practice 1

Beryl enters her colleague's room: his eyes are fixed on the computer screen.

Beryl:	'Have you got that research data I asked you about before?'

Colleague   *(his eyes still on the screen):* 'Uh huh, not yet.'
Beryl: 'Well, I want to talk to you. When are you going to do something about it?'

Beryl's learning 1

Never, never, never speak to anyone until you have their attention. In other words, wait until the person you are addressing is looking at you. As long as the other person is gazing at a computer screen, reading a newspaper, watching television or talking on the phone – in other words, giving their attention *elsewhere* – do not utter a word.

WAIT.

This often comes as a revelation to many women. The question to ask yourself is: when you speak to someone while they are otherwise engaged, what does that imply about what you have to say? The immediate answer is that what you are saying has no importance or relevance. It indicates to the other person that it is unnecessary to distract themselves from anything else to pay attention to what you are saying.

But it is so very hard to break this habit. Sometimes I think we get anxious and so talk on compulsively. Then we get irritated with the lack of response, which makes us even more anxious and so we keep talking... all a waste of words and effort.

So the first lesson here is to use the person's name and then *wait* until they look at you. Because they will. And if they look back to whatever they are doing, you keep quiet until they look back to you. Then you continue.

Practice 2

Beryl: 'Graham, I'd like to talk to you.'
Graham   *(eyes still on the screen):* 'Uh huh.'
Beryl: 'I'd like a word with you, Graham.'

Graham (eyes still on the screen): 'Go ahead.'
Beryl stays silent, tense and anxious, but resolutely silent.
Graham glances up at Beryl: 'What is it?'
Beryl: 'I would like to talk about...'
Graham looks back to the screen.
Beryl stops talking.
Graham looks up again.
Beryl: 'I would like to talk about the research data I have asked you for. And I would like you to listen to my request.'
She takes a deep breath and stands her ground.
Graham turns his body around to face her: 'What is it then?'
Beryl: 'I'd like you to look up that data for me. It's urgent now *(learning from other role-plays)* so can we agree on a time when you'll get back to me?'
Graham: 'I know, I just haven't got round to it. How about the end of the week?' He starts to turn back to the screen.
Beryl: 'Graham.' He turns back to look at Beryl. 'You'll let me have it by the end of the week. Can I rely on that?'
Graham: 'Yes, alright. The end of the week, I promise.'
Beryl: 'Thanks.' She leaves...

... collapsing in a cold sweat to our applause. 'It was so *hard,*' she said, 'not to say anything.'

Beryl's learning 2

It is hard. The prospect faces us with deep anxiety and the possibility of rejection but remaining silent, without filling the space with placating comments, compulsive mumblings or snide remarks, is an empowering experience. With practice, you will come to believe that even if your request isn't met, you are worth listening to and that your request is worth someone else's full attention, even if briefly.

Taking yourself seriously means being able to challenge

sometimes what you see and hear. We often hesitate to interrupt someone else because we have all, at times, experienced interruption as aggression and do not want to be rude. There are times when interrupting someone is necessary.

Handling interruptions

Katherine found herself feeling confused and frustrated in meetings where senior male academic staff droned on in a haze of muddled statements. No one else seemed to have a problem, so she began to assume that she must be the stupid one for not understanding.

Practice 1

Meeting in progress. The professor drones on. In her first attempt, Katherine kept trying to summon up the courage to speak, waiting for the right moment.

Katherine's learning 1

You have to direct your comments to the person concerned. 'How can I do that,' she asked, 'when he is so senior?' He may well be more senior, more this and more that, 'higher' in all sorts of ways, and yet he is being unclear. He may be sublimely unaware of this lack of clarity because nobody has ever told him directly.

The best starting point is the person's name.

Practice 2

Drone in progress.

Katherine: 'Professor Jacobson, I am sorry but...' spoken half in and half out of her throat, consequently inaudibly.

Katherine's learning 2

If you are interrupting to gain attention, you have to raise your voice accordingly. 'Won't that sound aggressive?' asks Katherine. The answer is that we often under-estimate the volume necessary to interrupt someone talking. Your voice need not be loud but it does need to be firm. Remember, too, not to apologize for the other person being unclear.

Practice 3

Drone in progress.

Katherine takes a deep breath: 'Professor Jacobson.' He stops talking and looks at her. 'I am finding it very difficult to understand what you are talking about. I don't know about anyone else, but I would be grateful if you would clarify this point for me.' (This she manages with a smile.)

Katherine's learning 3

The longer you wait, the harder it gets: the sooner you speak, the more chance you have of managing your anxiety.

Now let's look at what happens when *you* are the one being constantly interrupted.

Angela, a senior editor, presented a problem with a partic-ular male colleague whom she described as dominating, loud and aggressive in meetings. He would constantly interrupt while she was talking and she felt dismissed.

This sort of situation becomes a vicious circle. Our response to being interrupted is one of resentment or irritation and these feelings are hard for us to acknowledge. As time passes and the interruptions continue, the response is swallowed down repeatedly and we withdraw, not from fear but from anger. Handling an interruption *as it occurs* is therefore a useful skill to acquire.

Practice 1

In a meeting of a dozen colleagues, Angela starts to present her views.

Angela: 'This book is new and powerful and I think it should be our lead title for next...'

Gary (cutting across the group to another colleague, in a loud voice): 'I don't think it's our style ... Brian, what was the one you were mentioning to me...?'

Brian: 'The guy travelling with the Bedouin?'

Gary: 'Yes, that one. I think that would be the best bet, don't you?'

Angela is left sitting tight-lipped, alternating between fury and despair.

Angela's learning 1

How can Angela interrupt in return? What can she say? What words can she use without getting into an argument?
  Keeping it simple works better than trying to be clever:

'I'd like to finish my point.'

'I'd like to finish what I was saying.'

As with the previous role-play, using the person's name is the best starting place, spoken clearly and firmly to get his attention.

Practice 2

Angela: 'This book is important and I really think it should be our lead title for...'

Gary: 'I don't think it's right. Brian, what was the one you mentioned to me? Wasn't it a travelling story...?'

Angela (speaking quietly): 'Gary, I'd like to finish what I was saying...'
Gary continues talking to Brian without pausing. She waits.

Angela's learning 2

Angela is now finding it difficult to *make* an interruption and is waiting for Gary to finish. This may be polite, but in this situation it is ineffectual. Angela must interrupt early on while Gary is speaking and not wait until he stops. To do this, she has to raise her voice and, like Beryl before, repeat Gary's name until he stops talking and looks at her.

Practice 3

Angela: 'This book is excellent and new and I would like to see it as our lead title for...'
Gary: 'It's the wrong book for the lead title. Brian, what was the book...?'
Angela (taking a breath): 'Gary.'
Gary: '...that you mentioned last week...'
Angela (louder): 'Gary.'

Gary looks away from Brian and towards Angela.

Angela: 'I'd like to finish what I was saying.'
Gary: 'But I don't agree...'
Angela: 'I'd still like to finish what I was saying.'

The attention of the whole meeting is on Angela now. She looks away from Gary and around to the other members of the group and continues:

'I think it would be a good lead title and I'd like to know if anyone else agrees with me?'

Applause from us.

Angela's learning 3

This is much more difficult to do than first appears. Angela is learning to *manage* an interaction – not dominate or manipulate it – but manage her part in it. This is assertive communication. Making eye contact, using the person's name, getting their attention before speaking, redirecting your own gaze around the room and inviting a response are all aspects of this kind of management.

This approach may feel mechanical and awkward at first because it is new. With practice, you feel more comfortable and more confident. You know that you are taking yourself – your ideas, your opinions, your thoughts – more seriously and can take responsibility for expressing these in a manner in which they can be heard. It is being heard that is important, not necessarily being right. Others may disagree with you but they cannot agree or disagree if they haven't listened in the first place.

four

Feelings at work

What does managing anxiety mean? What is anxiety? Why do we feel it? Given that similar physical symptoms occur in response to anger, how do we know which emotion we are experiencing?

At this point in the course, we have to challenge the entrenched belief that feelings have no place in a working environment: that feelings are personal and therefore private and not appropriate in the workplace.

This, and the associated belief that we must at all times be *rational*, is pervasive. Yet management of feelings at work is one of the critical parts of these courses. Why? Because as long as humans rather than robots are employed, feelings will be an inevitable part of working life.

Imagine, for example, how you might *feel* when faced with the following situations:

☐ A third person cuts across you during an important discussion and takes over the conversation.
☐ Your boss contradicts your assessment of a situation and undermines your credibility with other colleagues.
☐ Someone repeatedly fails to follow your instructions.
☐ Your own hard work appears credited with someone else's name.
☐ Your colleague makes public something you told her in confidence.
☐ You experience conflict between the demands of your family and your career.
☐ You are criticized fairly or unfairly in public.

☐ Your contribution is devalued because you don't fit into an 'attractive young thing' stereotype.
☐ All the work and effort of your team is demolished by an arbitrary decision from on high.
☐ Your personal priority of care for your clients is dismissed as irrelevant and naïve.

Each of us would respond to the above situations with slightly different feelings, but we would all certainly feel *something*. So how can we manage feelings more effectively at work?

The concept of *managing* feelings is usually new to participants. Managing conveys a sense of order, structure and competence that sounds quite alien to the subject of emotion and yet this is precisely what we can learn to apply to our feelings. Most women carry around in their minds not only the 'no feelings at work' ethic but also many other stereotypes; these make us fear being seen as hysterical, emotional, manipulative, 'having problems', hormonally unbalanced: in short, unprofessional.

And yet it doesn't take much digging to bring to the surface a whole range of feelings – some mild, some very intense – so how do we learn to manage them? First of all, it helps to have some basic information about what feelings are and where they come from. The following explanation and description of feelings comes from my book *Trusting the Tides* (Rider Books, 2000), which is a comprehensive guide to the emotions. We look at a small part of the content to try and order some of the chaos with which we view the whole topic.

It is helpful to understand human emotions and feelings in the context of three polarities of human need, as these polarities are crucial in understanding the source of emotion; we will look at each in turn.

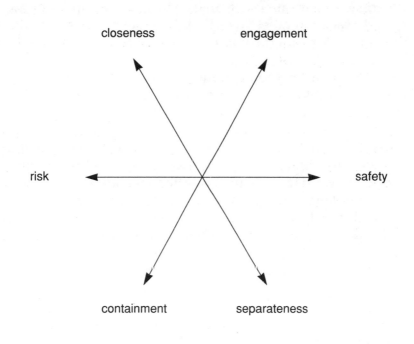

Figure 4.1

Closeness..Separateness

The needs for closeness and separateness are equally important at different times in our lives and we move between the
two needs depending on which is uppermost at any particular time. An infant needs nurture for emotional survival and
also needs to develop a separate sense of self. This toing and
froing between the two needs continues through childhood,
adolescence and into adulthood.

As adults, the need for intimacy includes giving and
receiving care and love in all its forms. There are times when
we want to be close, to be held, to share a happy or hard

experience. There are other times when we long to be alone, to find peace and quiet, to pull up the drawbridge and make time to clear out all the interpersonal clutter and get back to ourselves.

The need for love and closeness is more obvious to people than the need for separateness. More often than not we are encouraged and conditioned to regard only the first of these needs as significant. Many participants are surprised but relieved when this is pointed out because it answers the nagging but unspoken longing that they feel, without being able to put words to it. Many of us find that our daily lives are spent fulfilling the demands of all kinds of professional, parental, social and personal roles. Regardless of how willing and fulfilled we are in these different roles, there is still something missing. We forget, because we are not encouraged to remember, that we need and have a right to some time for separateness, a time to regain our own internal integrity and balance.

When the need for closeness or separateness is fulfilled, the emotions are based in love which includes feelings of joy, tenderness, contentment, happiness and warmth. The following examples give an idea of how our needs for closeness can be met in different ways in our lives. Clearly some are more relevant to our personal than professional lives:

Being listened to

Companionship

A smile of welcome

Preparing a loving surprise for someone

Receiving and giving praise

Support through a hard time

A shared endeavour

Being valued

The experiences that might fulfil our need for separateness include:

Going for a run

Finding a quiet place to sit for a while

Burying oneself in a newspaper

Working out in the gym

'Switching off' from a situation

Closing the door on everyone

Meditation

Listening to music

When our needs for closeness or separateness are not fulfilled, the spectrum of emotions ranges from sadness, loss and hurt to sorrow and grief. Examples of experiences that block our need for closeness are:

Withdrawal of someone close to us

Separation from one's loved ones

Excessive criticism

Endings

Rejection

Being unable to confide in someone

Feeling unsupported

Being ostracized

Our need for separateness is blocked when we experience the following:

Lack of *being* because of over-*doing*

Lack of privacy

Over-interference by partner, friends or colleagues

Lack of silence

Never being alone without it feeling lonely

Getting swamped by our different roles at work and home

Every minute of every day taken up with attention to others' needs

Always having to give an account of yourself

Next, we move to the second polarity.

Engagement...Containment

The needs for engagement and containment are again equally important at different times of our lives. The need for engagement describes the need to be stretched, matched, to feel one's limits through interaction with others: to experience the *self* as fully and as strongly as possible. The need for containment describes the complementary impulse: we can only truly experience our own boundaries when they clash with *other* boundaries. This is how we find our limits and negotiate them.

The first need pushes for self-expression and the second need demands self-limitation, requiring a firm structure within which to experience the restraint of the other. How does this work in practice?

You can see these complementary needs very clearly in childhood: the early needs to kick and struggle, requiring something to kick *against*. A hallmark of adolescent behaviour is often a defiance of structure and a wish to establish an identity different from parental or social norms in dress, music, choice of friends and so on. Yet, the boundaries – the actual restraint of parental dictates about when to be home and how to behave – are essential for this process to occur.

How are the needs for engagement and containment experienced in our lives? Our need to engage is met when we:

Fight injustice

Beat the system

Pass an examination

Overcome a difficulty

Enjoy a heated debate

Take the initiative

Take on a challenge

Make an impact

Our need for containment can be met by:

Agreeing to disagree

Honouring a contract

Acknowledging our limitations

Taking responsibility for ourselves

Bowing to someone else's will

Knowing when to let go

Putting someone else's need first

Giving in graciously

When these needs are met, we experience a different group of feelings. These include elation, excitement, joy, zest, pride, satisfaction and peace.

When these needs are blocked and unfulfilled in some way, different feelings emerge.

Experiences that block our need for engagement include:

Being bullied

Being labelled a failure in the system

Being the victim of any kind of oppression

Being unheard

Not being given a choice

Being ignored

Not being stretched enough

Being cheated

Experiences that block our need for containment include:

Someone changing the goalposts

Dishonoured contracts

Random punishment

Sexual harassment

Insufficient structure

Inconsistent rules and regulations

Unclear boundaries

Being seen as an object

When either of these needs is restricted or suffocated, our feelings are based in the emotion of anger: frustration, annoyance, irritation, fury, indignation and rage.

Finally, we come to the third polarity.

Safety...Risk

The need for safety encompasses the need that we have as humans for recognition, repetition, for routine and familiarity. We need to belong. We need to build our own sense of identity, to know who we are and where we are. This is because we have to make sense of and order the randomness of our environment as a foundation for developing trust.

The safety born of this trust is vital for us to develop emotionally and intellectually. Again this need is seen in infancy and right through our lives, changing and modifying along the way, but always present. The need for safety is complemented by our need for risk. There comes a point in our lives when the familiar becomes restrictive and routine feels like a rut. We realize at some level that we need a change and this is how the need for risk asserts itself. We find ourselves wanting to move on, make a change, take a gamble on something different and new, in other words, risking the unknown.

Our need for safety can be met by the following experiences:

Making a room/office/space your own

Being able to be yourself with others

Being part of a social/professional/peer group

Being recognized with a smile

Gaining confidence in a new skill

Finding the right words

A supportive arm around you when you feel vulnerable

Being told the truth

Our impulse to risk can be satisfied by:

Braving disapproval

Initiating difficult conversation

Speaking up to someone in authority

Going for a new image

Standing in the minority

Trying any new behaviour

Seeking a new environment when you feel in a rut

Learning a new skill

When these needs are met, we respond with feelings of relaxation, trust, confidence, security, ease, belonging and contentment.

What can interfere with our need for safety?

Living with unpredictable moods

Being unable to find the right words

Being identified by the colour of one's skin or the shape of one's body

The threat of redundancy

Being inadequately prepared

Insufficient information

Exclusion from a group

Anticipation of a hostile response

Some of the experiences that block our need for risk include:

Being over-protected

Being labelled stupid

Over-dependence on others' approval

The promotion of prejudice

The belief that there is only one right way

Allowing no room for mistakes

Being ridiculed for losing

Never having to take responsibility

The feelings that emerge when our needs for safety or risk are not fulfilled, or are interrupted in some way, are based in the emotion of fear: anxiety, worry, dread, panic, alarm, terror.

These three polarities explain the three major groups of feelings. I have described them in turn to make it easier to understand, but our actual *experience* of emotion is usually a mixture because any event can mean the fulfilment or interruption of several needs at once. The experience of unfair criticism can leave us feeling resentful because it is unjust – it could also trigger panic if the criticism is delivered in an aggressive manner; we might also find the criticism very hurtful.

So in learning to identify what you are feeling, remember that there may be more than one strand because we are responding emotionally to different needs being met or unmet. If you feel you are part of the group you work with, if you feel safe and able to trust others, you will also feel more valued and cared for and be able to engage more fully in the challenges that come your way.

Self-disclosure

The most important skill in relation to managing feelings at work (or anywhere else) that we learn and practise on a course is self-disclosure. Self-disclosure is not a heart-to-heart dialogue or an opportunity to confess all. It is not fancy, complex, artistic or clever. Self-disclosure is simply communicating the truth of whatever you are feeling by putting it into words. This description makes it sound so obvious and easy that you may wonder why it should be even described as a *skill*. But having taught this skill over many years, I know, first of all, how supremely effective it is; secondly, how amazed people are when they get the hang of it because they find it so useful; and thirdly, how very difficult it is to learn.

The reason why it is a difficult skill to learn is because we are much more accustomed to denying what we feel, out of habit and under the influence of the following anxieties:

'If I say what I feel, I'll give them more power over me' | 'I'll be more vulnerable' | 'I'll be labelled hysterical.'

Although it is true that there are times when it is wiser to keep quiet and more appropriate to do so, most of the time this anxiety is based on the cultural dismissal of 'emotional' as 'weak'.

In the workplace, especially, it is hard to accept that feelings can be brought into our conversation. It is important to distinguish here between using self-disclosure, ie naming specific feelings to make our communication more truthful and more effective, and undifferentiated emotional collapse. It is entirely possible to acknowledge anxiety and remain competent at the same time. Being more human strengthens your communication because you come across as more real.

Self-disclosure allows you to state the reality of what you feel and then to get on with what you need to get on with. It does not mean losing your temper, bursting into tears, or dwelling morosely on emotional topics.

'I might get it wrong.'

Fear of looking foolish discourages us from listening to our emotional wisdom and makes us reluctant to address feelings that might put us in a bad light. It also means that we tend to hold back until we imagine we are absolutely in the right. This quickly translates into self-righteousness: a guarantee that the other person will respond defensively.

'I can't find the words.'

Understandable – but practice really does help. The inability to find the words stems from years of denying and ignoring our emotions until they accumulate to a degree when they become unavoidable. You can learn to become more in touch with your feelings from the cues in your body – which is where feelings occur – not in your head.

'If I don't say anything, the problem will just go away.'

Highly unlikely.

The consequence of denying our feelings and letting them build up is that when we *do* decide to say how we feel, it is often when things have gone past a comfortably manageable level. We tend to defend ourselves against vulnerability by relying on self-righteousness and blame. So the understandable mistake that we make when beginning to use this skill is to *appear* to be expressing our feelings while, in reality, criticizing the other person:

'I feel that you have no right to say that.'

'I feel you shouldn't do that.'

'You make me feel miserable.'

'I feel that you're wrong.'

'You intimidate me.'

'I feel that you're insensitive.'

'You make me feel really small.'

Self-disclosure, on the other hand, lies in assuming *responsibility* for our feelings, which entails recognizing that whatever you are feeling cannot be blamed on someone else. This is why it is so difficult to do. It involves a *huge* shift in awareness: it goes so deeply against the conditioned grain to accept that what you are feeling is what you are feeling and that nobody has *made* you feel like that.

Individual responses to perception of another person's behaviour vary so much that we cannot simply attribute a feeling to a cause even though we find comfort in doing so. If someone treads on your foot, you might have a case for arguing they had caused you pain, but even then, your response would vary from others' responses to the identical action: outraged, apologetic, surprised, slightly put out or vengeful are some of the possibilities.

The skill of self-disclosure lies in being clear and honest and upright:

● Being clear.

Naming as specifically as possible improves with practice. At first, you will find that words like 'upset' come more easily than angry, that 'confused' hangs around for a while until the fog begins to clear, that you will almost certainly understate the intensity of what you are feeling. Blanket terms of 'rejected' or 'disappointed' or 'guilty' tend to block your ability to be more specific and express yourself more effectively.

● Being honest.

There is no point in saying you are 'a bit upset' when you are furious, or hurt when you are angry. Nor is this skill about saying what you think the other person wants to hear. Or what you think might prevent someone expressing anger towards *you*. It is simply about conveying your emotional truth as far as you can see it at the time. That is enough.

● Being upright.

Ultimately, fault and cause and blame become irrelevant. The aim of self-disclosure is to verbalize what you are feeling in response to your perception. Communicating your feelings without blame allows the other person to hear more clearly and the possibility of an *exchange* becomes far more likely.

Putting your feelings into words need not involve blame or apology. Self-disclosure is a way of taking responsibility for what you feel, simply stating the truth, without the need to be right or wrong. We often do get it wrong but the only chance we have of sorting out emotional issues in relation to another person is by communicating without blame and in the spirit of *informing* the other person. We can never make pronouncements with anything approaching absolute certainty. Emotional articulation is relative and an emotional response to a perception may be inaccurate or may conflict with someone else's perception. When you state your feelings, you have a chance to compare perceptions and then evaluate your own feelings in the light of this exchange.

Eventually feelings can be included as just one part of your ordinary communication – even at work – as unselfconsciously and as naturally as you communicate your ideas, your opinions or thoughts. It is important to remember that self-disclosure applies to *all* feelings, not just the so-called negative ones. Expressing pleasure, delight, excitement or satisfaction can also be relevant to communication at work. If we've concentrated here on expressing difficult feelings, it is because these are the ones that cause us most trouble.

Self-disclosure is useful both at the time you are aware of an emotional reaction and, in the longer term, when talking about past events or when wanting, for example, to clarify misunderstandings. Apart from opening up the possibility for emotional exchange, this skill also helps to release psychosomatic tension.

Release of tension

Self-disclosure is a vital part of short-term emotional management because it acts as a first and major form of release of tension. This is because until there is an acknowledgement and therefore acceptance of the feeling, whatever it is, the battle will continue between the body, which pushes to release the feeling, and the head which has learnt to keep everything battened down. The greater the pressure for the feeling to be expressed, the greater the counter-effort of the head to control and prevent expression; the greater the tension, the greater the pressure and so on. Self-disclosure acts in an extraordinary way to allow the mouth to articulate the feeling, forming a meeting point between the battling head and body: head and body become congruent, acting *together* instead of against each other, the head finding the language to translate the physical sensations of emotion.

At this point, the conflict eases. There is a felt release of psychosomatic tension, especially if the language conveys the feeling accurately. The arousal doesn't dissipate immediately if it is high, but once the conflict between body and mind stops, once we acknowledge and name the truth of what we are feeling, the struggle subsides and the tension becomes more manageable.

The option of longer-term management

The use of self-disclosure acts as a bridge between short-term emotional management and a longer-term approach. Its practice puts us very much in touch with our physical sensations and helps to correlate these sensations with a nameable feeling or emotion. Choosing to 'have it out' with the person concerned, talking things through with a close and trusted friend, or arranging to do this with a professional is an important and vital part of emotional management and an immense help.

The ability to express our feelings and deal with situations *at the time*, or a short while afterwards, is crucial to managing our feelings in every area of our lives. However, the reality is that we don't do this: we deny our feelings, we swallow them down and bottle them up for days, weeks, maybe years. The result is that most of us, as adults, have accumulated a backlog of unexpressed and unreleased feelings. This accumulation will make itself felt from time to time in our personal and working lives.

We recognize these moments as times when we feel particularly vulnerable, 'stressed', under pressure: the combined demands and circumstances of our personal and working lives push us to a point that is intolerable and something has to give.

Sometimes, a release of tension comes when we erupt, blow a fuse, spill out aggression and resentment onto other people. At other times, the tension is released through collapse: we succumb to all sorts of aches and pains and illnesses, experience mental and physical exhaustion and in extreme circumstances, we experience a breakdown.

Release of psychosomatic tension (in our minds *and* in our bodies) does occur temporarily, both when we erupt and when we retreat for a while. Unfortunately though, it is unlikely that we are any clearer afterwards about what exactly caused the accumulation and what the feelings were. This understanding and clarity come from a longer-term approach to managing emotion in our lives and is the subject of my book *Trusting the Tides*.

For now, we look at the specific relevance of the skill of self-disclosure in a working environment.

five

When the answer is 'No'

To understand why anxiety is difficult to manage at work (or anywhere else), we have to look a little at the cultural background.

We tend to inherit a cultural approach that splits everything into two: either/or, black/white, right/wrong, good/bad. The way we look at feelings is no exception so that we automatically and unthinkingly divide feelings into positive/negative. Anxiety is an excellent example of what we refer to as a negative emotion: we don't like it and we feel at the mercy of it because it appears to emerge even when we are not expecting it. So therefore we don't acknowledge it. We even feel ashamed of feeling anxiety, interpreting it as a sign of weakness and a failing.

When I introduce the skill of self-disclosure in a class, there is always immense resistance. And yet, little by little, with constant reinforcement and experience, participants come back time after time and tell me with undisguised astonishment that self-disclosure really does help to communicate more effectively even in very difficult situations.

The first area in which it helps us is establishing boundaries and making assertive refusals.

What kind of situations at work require us to say 'No'? Women can find it hard to refuse:

- [ ] Extra work.
- [ ] A request for leave.
- [ ] To make the coffee.
- [ ] To change an agreed contract.
- [ ] To be available all the time for clients.

☐ To be criticized in public.
☐ To fill in for other colleagues on a habitual basis.
☐ To run inappropriate errands for the boss.

The recipe for saying 'No' contains three ingredients: the request of the other person and your refusal are two of them. These two ingredients on their own will leave the other person unacknowledged. The refusal, whether forthright or subtle, will be experienced as *aggressive*, so in order to transform this into an assertive refusal, we need the skill of self-disclosure.

Sheila, a careers adviser, found it hard to say 'No' whenever she was asked to cover in the evening because a colleague had to go home to deal with a family situation. She felt guilty because she didn't have children and therefore didn't believe she had the right to say 'No'.

Practice 1

Colleague comes into Sheila's office.

Colleague: 'Look, I've got to go home at five to deal with the children. Could you do me a favour and cover for me this evening?'

Sheila remains silent and helpless.

Sheila's learning 1

The effect of anxiety and guilt about saying 'No' is to 'blank out' our minds: we cannot think or find the right words.

Practice 2

Colleague: 'Can you do me a favour? I've got to get home early tonight... could you cover the evening session for me?'

Sheila: 'No, Sarah. I can't do it tonight. Sorry.'

Sheila's learning 2

The tone in Sheila's voice was a little wooden and stiff; in other words, she didn't sound like herself. I asked her what she *felt* about saying 'No'.

Sheila: 'It's difficult because I don't have children.'
AD: 'What do you feel about saying "No"?'
Sheila: 'You get a reputation for saying "Yes", so they don't bother to ask anybody else.'
AD: 'What do you *feel* about it?'
Sheila: 'I feel she should ask somebody else for a change.'
AD: 'What do you *feel* about saying "No"?'
Sheila: 'I don't like saying "No", I suppose, I feel guilty.'

Finally we get to self-disclosure, which is the third and essential ingredient.

Practice 3

Again it is helpful to use the person's name.

Sarah: 'I really need you to do me a favour. I can't do the evening session. I have to get back for the children. Can you cover for me?'
Sheila: 'Sarah, I feel guilty (*self-disclosure*) about this but, no.'
Sarah: 'No? Why?'
Sheila: 'Look, I really find it hard to say no (*self-disclosure*), but I would prefer you to ask someone else this time.'
Sarah: 'Are you doing something this evening?'
Sheila: 'Nothing special but I'd rather get home.'
Sarah: 'Well, I suppose I could go and try Tom...'

Sheila's learning 3

To those of you reading this, it will be hard to imagine just how anxiety-provoking it is to say no assertively and directly.

It really requires an immense effort because, at first, it feels as if it is going completely against every conditioned grain in you. It is so much easier to say 'Yes', be indirect or shut yourself off from the other person's needs. Sheila learnt that using self-disclosure offers a balance between feeling for the *other* person – their plight, their needs, their wants – and for *your* limits. Self-disclosure, combined with the other two ingredients, transforms an aggressive, uncaring refusal into one that is assertive and caring.

Some refusals present no problem to us because we feel confident in refusing. Refusals are easier when we can use rules and valid excuses as justification: 'I'm sorry but it's in the regulations/departmental policy/someone else's decision, not mine.' An official line makes a refusal possible without having to take personal responsibility for saying no to someone.

It is this assumption of responsibility that makes us feel vulnerable. Reasons why we feel anxious about saying no at work might include:

'They'll think I am not up to the job.'

'He'll be angry.'

'I don't want to be rude.'

'They'll think I don't care.'

'I don't want to look mean.'

'I don't want to appear inadequate.'

'She'll tell everyone I'm a bitch.'

'They might not ask me again.'

'I don't want to be labelled unsociable.'

I believe that everyone has difficulty in saying 'No' at times: those who state they never have a problem are often unaware of being aggressive. An aggressive refusal allows us to cut off from any feeling regarding the other person, a 'toughen up and get it over with' attitude that prevails in the work culture.

The person on the receiving end experiences an aggressive and an assertive refusal quite differently, as group participants find out for themselves. An aggressive refusal conveys the message clearly but leaves the other person feeling disregarded, dismissed or overruled. An assertive refusal leaves the other person possibly disappointed, irritated or surprised but always knowing that their request has been *acknowledged*. This subtle but important quality makes the world of difference to the character of the environment in which people have to work together. A brusque authoritarian 'No' can generate grudges; a clear and respecting 'No' encourages respect and clear boundaries.

How we say 'No', how we set limits, is what will matter in the end. Given the nature of the world and given the changing role in gender, most women find setting limits hard to do assertively. Although this anxiety crops up in every area of our lives, our main concerns at work centre on wanting to avoid giving an impression of being inadequate, uncooperative, or simply being seen as *difficult*.

Pam, a lecturer, found it hard to say 'No' when asked in a meeting to take on extra classes. She was unable to think clearly enough to refuse her Head of Department at the time, and then felt resigned to a continuing overload of work. She knew that she had more than she could cope with but didn't want to appear inadequate.

Practice 1

HoD: 'Pam, I thought you might be able to take on this section for the next two terms. We're a bit pushed and there is no one else who can do it. It shouldn't involve too much work. Okay?'

Pam (*not knowing what else to say*): 'Well, I don't know really…' – the meeting moves on and she says nothing more.

Pam's learning 1

Pam found it hard to think straight because of the pressure and confusion. I suggested that she used the phrase 'I don't know' but in a much stronger manner, asking clearly for time to think about the request. This is a very useful strategy. I have found that there is nothing so important that you can't have one minute to consider how you want to respond. Often you require longer – an hour, a day or even a week – if it is a major decision. How you express this to the other person is going to be crucial.

Practice 2

HoD: Pam, I thought you might be able to take on this section for the next two terms. We're a bit pushed and there is no one else who can do it. It shouldn't involve too much work. Okay?'

Pam: 'No, I feel awkward about saying this (*self-disclosure*), but I don't know what my answer is. I am not sure I am able to take it on just now. I'd like to think about it and get back to you tomorrow morning. Is that all right?'

HoD (*surprised*): 'Well... is there a problem or something?'

Pam: 'It's not a problem really. It's just that it is an important issue and I'd like some time to think it over.'

HoD: 'Alright then ... but I can't see any reason why you can't do it.'

Pam's learning 2

Pam found it useful to ask for time to think. This strategy is very helpful because we cannot think clearly with a mind that is blurred with anxiety. I've found sometimes that when I am faced with a decision over the phone, even the action of putting down the receiver allows my confusion to diminish and my head to clear, so that it doesn't take long, from that stand-point, to know what my answer is.

We then went on to role-play the situation of Pam going to give her response to her HoD. I asked Pam why she wanted to say 'No' and she said it was because she had too much else to do and was struggling as it was. The image of struggling is quite damaging for self-esteem. It implies subtly that the struggle is our fault in some way and that we wouldn't need to struggle if we were more competent. Here lies a basic, fallacious but pervasive myth of Superwoman.

The many hundreds of women with whom I have worked over the years are outstandingly, extraordinarily, inspirationally *hard* workers, often, it must be said, working more productively than their male counterparts. And yet, Superwoman sits on our shoulders, driving us on with fears of inadequacy and never urging us with appreciation of our efforts so we tend always to find ourselves lacking, deficient in some way. With some preparatory work on this theme, it was possible for Pam to see that setting a limit on the amount of work she could do *effectively* was a positive rather than a negative gesture.

Practice 3

Pam enters Head of Department's office.

HoD: 'Oh hello, Pam, what can I do for you?'

Pam: 'I'd like to talk to you about what you asked at the meeting yesterday.'

HoD: 'I remember. Sit down.'

Pam: 'I feel anxious saying this (*self-disclosure*), because I don't want to appear inadequate, but I've given it a lot of thought and I'd like to say no to taking on the extra curriculum.'

HoD: 'What's the matter? I don't understand what the problem is.'

Pam: 'Nothing's the matter, it's just that I have got enough on my plate, having taken on the extra class last year as well and I am worried that if I take on more, I won't be able to do justice to my current teaching, let alone the new content.'

HoD: 'Well, if you put it like that, I suppose you have got a lot on... do you have any ideas who else could do it?'

Pam: 'I'm not sure, I'll have to think about it. I must go now. I've got a class at 10 o'clock.' She gets up to leave the room. 'I'll call you this afternoon.'

Pam's learning 3

Once she had transformed the fear of inadequacy into a realistic and true concern, Pam felt much more confident about this approach. She still felt anxious about stepping out of her familiar, compliant role but was able to manage by using self-disclosure. Feeling more certain about her reason gave her confidence to stand alongside her anxiety.

Sometimes, we find it hard to say 'No' because we don't want to make a fuss. Stella had risen from a secretarial post to an administrative/managerial post but she explained that her boss hadn't quite made the transition in his mind: he would frequently interrupt her work to ask her to make cups of coffee whenever he had visitors as he had done before.

She had reminded him of her new responsibilities once or twice, but he seemed to 'forget'.

Practice 1

Boss (putting his head around the door of Stella's office): 'Stella, could we have four teas when you have a moment?' He disappears.

Stella looks at me and shrugs her shoulders helplessly.

Stella's learning 1

Some situations are best handled when you turn them on

their heads, in other words, instead of waiting for them to happen again, you can *take the initiative.*

Whenever you want to address a habit of saying 'Yes' when you mean 'No', it is a tremendous help to take the initiative. This is for three reasons:

1. Saying 'No', at the moment of being asked, puts us on the spot and often makes us defensive. We risk saying 'Yes' again, or being aggressive. Confronting the difficulty before it reoccurs helps us to handle it more calmly.
2. Taking the initiative helps you prepare the other person for a change in your usual behaviour. This is important because the person making the request is likely to be unaware that you have wanted to refuse in the past ... because you have never done so. Alerting them to a coming change avoids being punitive.
3. Having alerted the other person and made them aware of your own difficulty, it then becomes easier to say 'No' on the spot because your refusal will have a context instead of simply coming out of the blue.

Practice 2

In preparation, I suggested that Stella make the time to speak to her boss.

Stella enters his office and sits down.

Geoff: 'Yes, Stella, you wanted to see me.'

Stella: 'I do, Geoff. I feel a bit silly about bringing this up (*self-disclosure*), but it is important to me. You often ask me to make cups of tea and coffee for your visitors, and I would like to stop doing this because it interrupts my work.'

Geoff: 'You always appear quite happy to do so.'

Stella: 'I know, it is hard for me to say "No", but I really would prefer you either to make it yourself or to ask someone else.'

Geoff: 'All right then. I am sorry if I have offended you ...' (*a slight dig*)

Stella: 'No, I am not offended. It's just that in the future, I may have to say no to you and now we've talked about it you'll understand why.'

She then looks at me awkwardly, and I signal to her to get up and go.

Stella's learning 2

It's important to get up and leave as soon as the interaction is over. This is difficult to do because whenever we behave in a different way, whenever we say something that is unfamiliar to us, the natural and healthy response is anxiety. After the conversation is over, we tend to feel a bit uncomfortable and uncertain about what to say or do next. There is a risk that we sit or stand waiting for permission to leave, so you have to force yourself to get up or walk away, however hard it is to do.

This is why these courses are so much about managing your anxiety instead of waiting until you feel confident enough to make that first move ... because you are likely to be waiting forever. Once you recognize anxiety and acknowledge it, you can still function with the feeling, instead of suppressing it, avoiding it or denying it. Self-disclosure helps defuse anxiety very effectively.

Many times after a course, women ask: 'I can manage to say no now but can you tell me how to do it without feeling anxious/dreadful/guilty?' My answer is that I believe it is impossible to make an assertive refusal without feeling some anxiety, if not at the time then an hour or a day afterwards. Robots can say 'No' without feeling anything but if you are human, and want to keep all three ingredients – acknowledgement of the request, self-disclosure and a clear 'No' – in your refusal, then you will feel anxious. And when you do feel fearful or guilty after setting limits in a difficult situation, remember that these feelings are simply a measure of how hard it was for you to say 'No' in the first place. Try giving yourself a pat on the back for courage instead of a rap on the knuckles for weakness.

six

Setting limits at work

As a useful background to this part of the course, I use the diagram shown in Figure 6.1, which helps to explain why setting limits is difficult. The upper half of the diagram refers to the more traditional stereotype of qualities that are felt to be attractive in a woman's behaviour and disposition. The lower half describes other, equally important aspects of being human that, in reality, often conflict with the expectations above. The encouragement to be nurturing, caring, concerned and sensitive pulls in one direction. Pulling in the opposite direction are our needs to be separate, to remember who we are under all our roles and responsibilities; our personal needs for care, support and renewal.

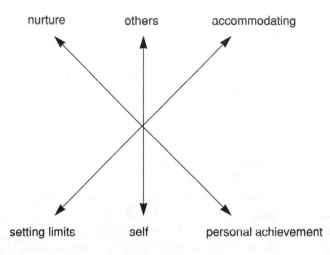

Figure 6.1

The awareness of others dictates most of our waking moments: what *others* want, what we imagine or anticipate *others* might want, what *others* think of us, how *others* approve or disapprove of us, how *others* might be affected by what we say and do. On the opposite side is the focus on *self*: What do *I* want? What are *my* thoughts, feelings, needs, beliefs, opinions?

The need to be caring, combined with the awareness of others, inclines us towards accommodation: not sometimes but *always* trying to be all things to all people. We push ourselves to physical and emotional limits to accommodate others' needs and, in the process, we can lose sight of our own. This is the relevance of setting limits, which simply means placing a boundary that can be flexible but firm enough to know where we begin and end and where others begin and end.

This is one of the most vital lessons of the course and the skills of assertiveness are very helpful here. When you look at the diagram you may be able to identify with the pull between the top half and the lower half, a pull that is internal but also reflected in external experience. The culture that promotes an either/or approach encourages us to choose between being a proper mother and a real career woman, for example, implying that the two are incompatible. More and more, these days, women find themselves trying to be Superwoman, achieving a successful career and a happy husband and family.

There is often a heavy cost, both physically and psychologically, to achieving Superwoman status. Not every woman wants to push herself to the extremes of going into labour while simultaneously clinching a multi-million pound deal. I find that the reality for most working women is that they want to succeed and achieve at work whilst *still* retaining their nurturing, caring qualities. They do not want to sacrifice their hearts on the altar of competition and profit.

Clearly these pulls and pushes reflect the difficulty we have in setting limits in every area of our lives. I was brought up to believe that if I cared for someone, I could not say 'No' to them: that one reality automatically cancelled out the other. When we do want to set limits while still respecting and/or caring for the other person, an assertive approach helps us to manage more effectively the conflict between the two realities.

Jill worked as a therapist in a drug abuse centre, and found it difficult to handle a particular client who would make personal comments about her that made her feel uncomfortable. Her conflict was that she needed his trust in order to work together, but she felt personally compromised by his questions.

Practice 1

Jill: 'So, Dave, how have you been doing this week?'
Dave: 'Much better. I am really getting myself together now… You're looking good today. Nice tan you're getting. Been sunbathing? (*Looking hard at her.*) How's your boyfriend?'
(*Jill is stumped and doesn't know what to say.*)

Jill's learning 1

I asked Jill what she was feeling. Her response was a mixture: confusion, anxiety and irritation. She didn't want to be rude or alienate him but she felt embarrassed.

Practice 2

Jill: 'So, Dave, how have you been doing this week?'
Dave: 'Great, doing a lot better now… applied for a job. You're looking good today… nice skirt, shows your legs off…'
Jill: 'Dave, listen a minute… I really don't like you making personal comments. Can we change the subject?' (*Her tone of voice is sharp.*)

Dave is surprised and uncomfortable. An awkward atmosphere is left between them.

Jill's learning 2

Once you have said what it is you want to say, and you have used self-disclosure, you have to move on, to change the subject and close that part of the conversation.

Practice 3

Jill: 'So, Dave, how have things been this week?'
Dave: 'Great, doing a lot better with everything now... you're getting a nice tan. Is it all over?'
Jill: 'Dave, I want to say something to you. I feel uncomfortable when you make personal comments (*self-disclosure*). I know you're being friendly, but I'd prefer to keep our conversation directed towards you. You're the important one here.What job did you apply for?' (*Deliberately switching the focus to safer and more appropriate ground.*)

Jill's learning 3

In acknowledging your feelings you can also acknowledge the other person as an equal. Others do not always know how their behaviour is affecting you, so keeping out blame helps maintain the equality of the interaction. Moving on and changing the subject is important for *both* of you.

The long-term value of setting limits

When we focus on the difficulty of setting limits, we often uncover a painful struggle between a real self and a conditioned self. This emerges as we discover that we often experience an internalized conflict:

- what we want vs. what we think we *should* want;
- what we feel vs. what we *ought* to be feeling;
- what we believe vs. what we are *expected* to believe;
- what we don't want vs. what *should* be acceptable.

The prescribed desires and feelings reflect our attachment to others, to external reference points, whether actual individuals in our lives, or images and stereotypes.

Ultimately, we have to acknowledge the truth in ourselves. Setting limits begins to build different psychic muscles, so instead of referring to others all the time, you start to build an internal reference point: yourself.

☐ What do I really want?
☐ What do I really feel?
☐ What do I really see?
☐ What do I really believe?
☐ What are my real limitations?
☐ How far am I prepared to accommodate?

All of these considerations enable us to make the first steps towards a place of *choice*. Making empowering choices as an adult stands in contrast to the passive and helpless option of a victim or the oppressive option of oppressing or controlling others.

There is much in life that we have no choice over, but how we behave, the words we speak, the attitude with which we engage with others are all open to choice. To choose, we need to learn what our options are: when we ignore the choices that we do have – either because we feel too anxious to confront the situation or because we don't know how to behave differently – we end up feeling powerless.

When we don't set limits, not once or twice but habitually, what happens?

When we want to say:

'No.'

'Enough.'

'I don't like this.'

'I don't agree.'

'My needs are important as well.'

and instead we say:

'Yes.'

'Fine.'

'I don't really mind.'

'Whatever you say.'

'My needs don't count.'

what are the consequences?

In the short term, what happens is immediate relief. The anxiety elicited by the immediate conflict – between the need to be caring and the need to set limits to that caring – diminishes. We have kept the boat from rocking and stabilized it on course again. The crisis is over. The status quo is restored. The risk of disapproval and uncertainty has been avoided. We remain as pleasing and accommodating as usual.

In the long term, however, I have seen many insidious consequences in professional and personal relationships, in my own life, and in those of the individuals I have worked with. There is an inevitable accumulation of irritation, resentment, bitterness, blame, anger and depression. Often an overwhelming sense of powerlessness can lead to withdrawal, going through the motions, half-hearted efforts. We find ourselves lost in confusion where problems in our lives loom out of the fog and appear alarming and insurmountable. No relationship – whether at work or at home, with children, family, parents, colleagues, friends, partners – is immune to the virus of accumulated resentment and its consequences.

Setting personal limits happens when you say no. It happens when you state where you stand on any issue, when you express what you feel, when you make a clear request. So what are the consequences? What happens if we sometimes say 'Enough is enough'; when we acknowledge to ourselves and others 'Beyond this point is unacceptable to me'?

In the short term we undoubtedly feel a huge increase in anxiety as well as the possibility of guilt, self-doubt, awkwardness and loneliness. We have to face and deal with other people's surprise sometimes, their confusion, perhaps their disapproval or displeasure and occasionally rejection. In the long term, however, a gradual but unmistakable process begins. With encouragement to survive the hard times, this process, once initiated, can never really be halted.

First, we notice an increased sense of clarity. The notion of choice becomes a familiar concept. Once you can exercise more choice in saying 'No', you can even say 'Yes' more comfortably to demands you'd prefer not to meet if you only had yourself to think about. The difference is that instead of meeting a demand grudgingly, you can do so more willingly, even if it is an obligation. Exercising more choice in some parts of your life helps you to be more accepting at times when there really is no alternative other than to acquiesce and yield to circumstances beyond your control.

As this process unfolds, you find that instead of the imagined selfish and nasty stereotype emerging, your ability to care for others and to respect others as equals actually becomes more heartfelt and more authentic. You also find yourself becoming more aware of others' limits and more respectful of other people's refusals. This can allow you to make your own requests more directly instead of trying to control and manipulate the answer. Setting limits allows others to respect you more because they know where they stand with you in a personal or professional role. This builds real confidence and genuine trust.

As the process becomes more established and familiar, you also begin to value your time more highly. Sometimes others, too, learn to value your time more highly as a consequence. You realize that time is the most precious commodity we have in life and that how we use it is vital.

seven

Being angry not aggressive

Among all the feelings, I find there is a particular interest in knowing how to manage the emotion of anger. When participants have begun to look at their situations at work or at home in which they feel most powerless, they realize that under the pile of rubble made up of put-downs, unfair criticisms, unappreciated efforts, being ignored, overlooked, taken for granted, not speaking up, not being taken seriously, being passed over, being patronized, thwarted, rendered invisible, or belittled... there is perhaps a little anger. Just a touch!

We have to begin by stating fairly and squarely that the situations women find themselves resentful of are usually 50 per cent their responsibility. In other words, because we do not make clear requests, because we do not set clear limits, because we do not exercise the choices that we do have, we end up with situations to which we have contributed unawares.

This does not mean at all that nothing can be done, but it does mean that we have to work hard to keep out blame. In short, we have to look very carefully at the difference between anger and aggression. As I explained in Chapter 5, the emotion of anger and associated feelings of irritation, frustration and resentment are associated with the second polarity of need, the complementary needs for engagement and containment. When these needs are interrupted or blocked in some way, we experience anger.

Anger is a healthy, natural response to the experience of being cheated, invaded, deceived, treated unfairly, to the experience of having no choice. Anger is a healthy and natural response to effort being wasted, goalposts being changed, being excluded from information, being denied resources, being overlooked for promotion, being the object of unwanted physical or verbal harassment. Both too little structure and too much structure can make us angry.

Most of us learn when growing up that anger is negative, bad, dangerous and unacceptable. Most girls learn that anger is unfeminine and unattractive. We learn to simply swallow it back and deny it, doing our best to eliminate it from our emotional repertoire.

When looking at how to *manage* anger and use it as a dynamic energy in our lives, we have to look first at the habitual ways in which we express this emotion. Stereotypically 'angry' behaviour is usually described in the following ways:

Abusive (verbally or physically)

Arrogant

Loud

Hysterical

Out of control

Hurtful

Violent

This is a familiar description of 'anger' – but it is entirely wrong. This is, in fact, a picture that illustrates *aggression*, one of the behavioural responses to anger.

Aggression is separate from the emotion itself. *Anger is a natural emotion, while aggression is a learnt behavioural response.* We learn when young to behave aggressively and this learning is reinforced in every aspect of our lives. Work is no exception. Aggression has become normal, accepted, expected behaviour. But it is not the genuine article. The intention behind aggression is to:

Blame

Defeat

Punish

Score

Crush

Humiliate

Win

Aggression is misleading because it is often a defensive response to fear, anxiety, to a sense of powerlessness. The key to aggression is blame. When anger is unexpressed, the accumulated emotion roves around seeking a target for blame. Once we identify this behaviour as aggressive, we can then identify other kinds of behaviour through which anger emerges when unacknowledged and unexpressed.

Another recognizable behaviour pattern is indirect aggression. The intention – to blame – is the same but it is less obvious and less loud; it involves less open confrontation and more behind-the-scenes activity. We see this expressed in the following kinds of behaviour:

Sarcasm

Put-downs

Gossip

Deflating comments

Sabotage

Passing on 'second-hand' criticism

Non-verbal gestures, for example: raised eyebrows, a pat on the head, a squeeze of the cheek, a smirk

The intention is again to blame, defeat, punish, score, crush, or humiliate; in short, to *win*.

In the previous examples, the intention is directed towards someone else. A third, familiar pattern of behaviour which stems from unexpressed anger is when this intention is directed inwards: we blame ourselves. We believe, consciously or unconsciously, that the fault, the inherent defect, the fundamental flaw must lie *within*.

The inwardly-directed blaming is expressed in the following ways:

Self put-downs

Self-negating beliefs

Constant moaning

A victim stance

Self-defeating behaviour

Self-mutilation

Self-punishment

Harmful eating/working/smoking/drinking habits

Addictive behaviour

Depression

Suicide attempts

Managing anger safely and effectively

The problem many of us face with anger, as in fact with all of our emotions, is one of accumulation. Clearly, our feelings don't travel along entirely separate paths. They are all interwoven: when they are stimulated, when we experience them, when we express them, and when we release them.

However, the build-up of anger makes us more determined than ever to keep the lid on tight because we fear for the consequences. Most of us do erupt when the pressure gets too much: sometimes at the wrong person, sometimes at the wrong time, and sometimes at the right person who is shocked at being suddenly demolished by all that we have been saving up.

Even if we are convinced that we have *good reason* to be angry, the backlog will distort our clarity, and it is likely that our need to offload will result in the 'target' experiencing not only the anger that he or she has triggered, but a whole lot more into the bargain. When it comes to this point, we don't really care in the heat of the moment, but we do later on. Remorse sets in and as we pick over the pieces of rubble we resolve never to do this again and things quieten down ... until the next time.

In the last chapter we looked at the problem of setting limits or boundaries. Managing anger means first acknowledging it as a healthy emotion which tells us when our boundaries are encroached.

Establishing clearer boundaries is an essential aspect of empowerment. All the areas described so far relate to this central concept of establishing a base of personal power. Consistent failure to make requests, express feelings, say 'No' and set limits leaves our personal boundaries indistinct under a haze of confusion and resentment. We end up experiencing our boundaries only when other people clumsily, repetitively and habitually invade them.

When someone asks us to do something extra, for example, often our immediate response is resentment:

'What do they think I am doing already?'

'Why can't they see?'

'How can he ask for more all the time?'

'Doesn't she understand that I have enough to cope with?'

Grumble, grumble, seethe, seethe, seethe.

And yet how is anyone to discover the limits of another – in

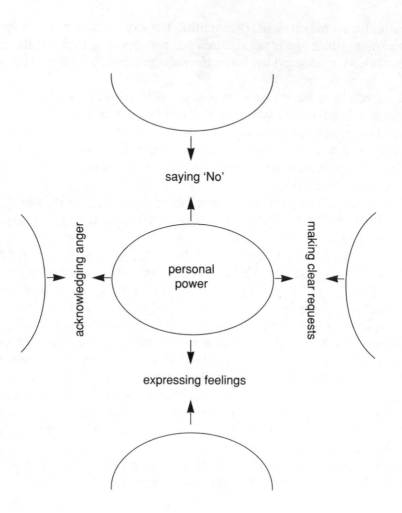

Figure 7.1

whatever relationship – unless they are clearly informed?
Managing anger is about informing another person when
enough is enough:

● When the limit has been breached.
● When a barrier has been crossed.

- When your choice has been taken away.
- When your need for structure and support is unfulfilled.
- When your need for a reciprocal relationship is unmet.

Reciprocity is about being mutual. Mutuality is about being equal. Assertive behaviour is about being equal. I believe that fundamentally, as humans, we want to give *and* take, we want criticism and praise, we want our efforts valued and used, we want an exchange, we want constraints to work within as a challenge, not as a prison.

Managing anger assertively has two equally important dimensions that should *never* occur at the same time: communication and release.

- Communication.

Blame will have to be put aside. You can put it on a comfortable cushion or in the drawer or just outside the door so it doesn't feel forgotten entirely but *do not* bring it with you into the interaction. If you do, however sweetly you smile or softly you speak, however assertive you imagine you are being, the underlying aggression (blame) will leak through the tone of your voice or gestures and is guaranteed to be picked up and responded to with aggression from the other person.

Valerie had an important management meeting with two colleagues for one hour a week. The problem for her was that they both left their mobile phones switched on: the constant interruptions and loss of meeting time made her furious. The more often it happened, the more frustrating it became. Her current way of communicating her feelings was to seethe throughout the meeting, send disapproving glances across the table, and then moan about it to someone else.

Practice 1

In the meeting, the mobile phone rings and colleague 1 responds to it. When she finishes, Valerie starts:

Valerie: 'Look, I have got to say something, do you think you could leave your phones switched off just for *one hour*? Surely that's not too much to ask? We do have things to get done, you know.'

Valerie's learning 1

In the feedback, she was told that her tone of voice came across as 'superior' and sarcastic. This happens very often: when we are angry we tend automatically to speak down to people. This is a knee-jerk response of aggression, because we think the only positions we have are up or down, right or wrong. Speaking from the 'right' position will always provoke a defensive reaction in the other person, even if this is not voiced at the time.

We have all experienced being told off by parents and teachers so we find it hard to express anger without this same superior approach creeping in, but with practice, we can make it more equal.

Practice 2

This time I suggested that Valerie spoke before the meeting started. This is because when we wait for the particular trigger that is making us angry, we make it much harder to keep at bay the accumulated feelings from past experience.

Two colleagues enter the room.
Valerie: 'Hi! Before we start I would like to say something. I feel a bit awkward about this but I get very irritated when your phones interrupt our meetings. We only have an hour and we have a lot to get through, so I wonder if you would agree to switching them off for the hour that we meet?'
Colleague A   (*a little surprised but open to Valerie's request*):

'Okay then, I may need to leave it on if there is a big event, but otherwise I don't mind.'

Valerie   (*to Colleague B*): 'How do you feel about it?'

Colleague B: 'I don't mind. I'm just wondering why you didn't say anything earlier.'

Valerie's learning 2

Her colleague's question at the end taught Valerie that unless you express what you feel, *the other person is unlikely to guess.* We do such a good job of dissembling that although we believe that he or she must know that something infuriates, annoys, enrages us or drives us around the bend, this belief is usually quite incorrect.

Denise discovered, when she saw the plans for relocation of office premises, that her particular needs had been over-looked. At the time she wished (as we do) that the authorities could have valued her work enough not to put her in the middle of an open plan office which was clearly unsuitable for the nature of her work as a student counsellor, which required privacy.

Over the ensuing weeks, she had approached various people to discuss this difficulty but no one had responded definitively. The move was made and she was now in the new location alternating between despair and fury, and considering looking for another post.

We worked out a strategy: identifying one person she could meet with and making an appointment to see her.

Practice 1

Sitting in the office of the accommodation registrar.

Denise starts: 'I've come to see you because, since the move, I have to work in totally unsuitable conditions. I don't know how I'm expected to do my job and nobody seems interested in doing anything to help.'

Denise's learning 1

Don't whinge. It turns people off. You can't expect anyone to know what it has been like or, in a work situation, even to care particularly. You have to be precise, specific and direct. It will certainly help you to acknowledge and express your feelings of frustration to yourself and possibly someone outside the situation, but when it comes to making a request like this, you need to keep out the moans and complaints, and stick to clear self-disclosure.

Practice 2

Denise: 'I've made this appointment because I want a change in my work location. I have asked for help before, unsuccessfully, and now I am feeling angry at being put in a position where I cannot work effectively. The students cannot relax without privacy and my job has become impossible. I would like some concrete action to be taken to find somewhere more suitable. What do you suggest?'

Denise's learning 2

From the other person's feedback in the role-play, Denise realized how much stronger her tone was and how much easier it was to respond to a clear request. Communicating in this way helped her to see how her needs could be taken seriously in this direct form, and not be so easily dismissed as an irksome complaint.

Both these examples highlight the need to take responsibility for your part in any interaction. Taking responsibility for past omissions is not the same as self-blame: it is simply an acknowledgement that you didn't speak up, that you didn't express what you felt. Why not? Because you didn't know how, you were afraid of the response, you didn't want to risk damaging the relationship, you didn't want to be misunderstood, you didn't know how to handle it differently. Now you do.

● Release.

The second dimension of expressing anger assertively is release. When this is discussed among participants, all sorts of personally helpful methods (used away from work) come to light: screaming, having a good yell, playing loud music, singing loudly in the car, doing housework with a vengeance, writing out all your murderous thoughts uncensored in a letter (but not posting it afterwards), going for a walk or a run.

Because of the constraints of professional life it is unlikely that any of us can release anger at the time. It would be inappropriate to do so. There are all sorts of ways of suppressing feelings in the short term: counting to 10, keeping a small towel in your desk drawer so that you can roll it up and scream into it in the privacy of the loo. (If you roll it up into the size of your wide-open mouth, you can yell quite freely and the sound will be suitably muffled.)

At other times, self-disclosure is useful. 'I feel so angry about this that I can't think or speak clearly at the moment'; you can leave the room, put down the phone or walk away and give yourself enough time to calm down before you say anything. These are assertive and empowering ways of managing anger.

Anger is a powerful, energetic emotion and will never be released through tears. Tears often precede the expression of anger, usually because of the accumulation of emotion. You feel choked and tearful, but tears are a different form of release: tears release feelings of sorrow, loss and hurt, so no amount of crying will ever release the emotion of anger. The actual chemicals in the body, produced by the arousal of the emotion, need to be released at some point. Release in your own private time and in a safe place needs to be vigorous, with movement and sound. Anger is a large emotion and, unlike the release of grief and fear, needs space and volume. Release of anger is short lived: it is released quickly and powerfully when allowed its natural process and rhythm. It is only unexpressed anger that rumbles on and on for a long time.

These two dimensions of management, communication and release, are equally important whichever comes first. Without *communication*, there is no opportunity to effect a change in your environment because the other person will not be informed. Although there are many times when we are powerless to effect change, there are also many situations in our lives where change is possible if we take an assertive approach.

On the other hand, without *release*, we risk not ever being clear enough to communicate. This is partly because of the backlog already described. Losing one's temper, seeing red, blowing a fuse, describe a state of body and mind that is an altered state because of the arousal of the emotion. We cannot think or see clearly because of this arousal. Even if what you are trying to communicate is correct, the other person is unlikely to heed what you are saying because most of us, when confronted with a loud barrage of words, are not able to listen, precisely because of the volume, and shut down instead to protect ourselves.

This does not mean that assertive expression of anger needs always to be polite and softly spoken. The tone of voice can be strong and effective but we will only manage this either before matters escalate or after the heat of the moment has passed. Once the arousal has diminished we are able to think clearly again and this is what helps us to keep out aggression and blame, but still be focused and direct in what we are choosing to communicate.

Lynne, a senior manager in a charity organization, described a particular problem with a much younger employee, Tanya, who did not turn up to meetings.

She said that every time she approached Tanya, her response was aggressive, and she couldn't get anywhere.

Practice 1

Lynne goes to see Tanya in her office.

Lynne: 'I'd like to talk to you, Tanya. I've just come from a meeting with Alan that you were meant to attend and I'd like to know why you weren't there.' *(All this was said in an angry manner, with 'headmistress' overtones.)*

Lynne's learning 1

Lynne was surprised when I described her manner. We are often unaware of how easily we slip into parental/teacher positions when we are cross with someone. Unfortunately, this only serves to re-stimulate the child/pupil counterpart in the other person, who will respond to the experience of being 'told off' with indirect or direct aggression.

I suggested that instead of going hot foot from the meeting to Tanya's office, Lynne looked at the difference between release and communication. She was understandably furious, and needed to let off steam. Taking time to calm down a little would make the interaction easier to manage.

Practice 2

Lynne approaches Tanya in her office.

Lynne: 'Tanya, I'd like to talk to you for five minutes.'
Tanya: 'If it's about the meeting…'
Lynne: 'Tanya, I'd like you to listen a moment. You agreed to meet with Alan and me at 12 and it was an important meeting. Because you didn't turn up, the time was completely wasted.'
Tanya: 'Well, something came up that I had to go to…'
Lynne: 'Something always comes up…'

Lynne's learning 2

A much better start and the absence of any patronizing tone came across as more effective. Now she needs to make the communication more complete. She needs to:

Use self-disclosure

Describe the behaviour that has made her angry

Make a specific request for change

Practice 3

Lynne: 'Tanya, I'd like to talk to you. I am absolutely furious (*self-disclosure*) because you didn't turn up to the meeting at 12 with Alan and me (*describing behaviour that made her angry*). I hate wasting my time (*self-disclosure*) and I would like to arrange another meeting that you'll make a commitment to come to, so that this doesn't happen again (*specific request for change*).'

Lynne's learning 3

The feedback was that Lynne's communication this time was clear, very angry and very powerful. There was no aggression coming from her, so Tanya felt confronted but not told off. She felt she had to take Lynne seriously.

Standing up in a storm

When responding to something that feels like a thunderbolt coming out of the blue, it is enough and often wiser not to communicate anything until you have had time to consider your position and to clear some of the immediate turmoil. Josie recounted an incident when she had been summoned to see her director and informed that the project on which she and three colleagues had been working hard for two years had been axed, the decision made over her head without consultation or consideration.

These incidents occur often in large organizations as corporate policy changes are implemented and human beings treated as objects, in a manner that is nothing short of abusive. The experience of powerlessness is real and inevitable. The only small but important thing we can do (for ourselves) is to state our anger clearly even though it is easier to remain silent.

Josie practises an alternative to being silent.

Practice 1

Director: 'I thought you'd better know that the project has been axed. Pity, I know, but that is the way it goes. You'll be transferred to research, probably. We'll let you know when we can. Is that okay?' *(Indicating an end to the conversation.)*

Josie had said nothing at the time because she was so shocked. This time she used self-disclosure

Josie: 'No, it's not okay... I'm really shocked... I'm devastated by what you've just told me... *(looking at the director)* I'm very angry at the waste of all our work.'

She takes a deep breath and gets up from her chair. 'Good afternoon,' she says awkwardly, but manages to leave his office.

Josie's learning 1

Josie expressed her amazement at the effect of having said *something* even though she felt awkward and inarticulate. She hadn't anticipated that it would make any difference. It didn't make any difference to the outcome, of course, but it made a difference to her self-esteem. She said that simply because she hadn't remained silent and invisible, which she felt implied that she deserved to be treated in that way, meant that she felt taller somehow when leaving the room.

Defusing aggression

One final aspect of this subject is how to respond more effectively to someone else's anger, even when, as is likely, it emerges as aggression. Remember that aggression is usually a knee-jerk response to fear, especially for men who have been culturally conditioned to react in this way.

Priti described an occasion when her boss burst into the office when she was talking to two colleagues and, standing in the doorway, berated her for giving him the wrong insurance figures in a review.

Practice 1

When we are shouted at aggressively we feel intimidated and frightened. I asked Priti to see if she could identify when this happened, as this would be our starting point.

'The boss' launches his attack. Priti responds as she did before (completely silenced).

Priti's learning 1

Priti identified feeling shocked; what did she want to say? She replied that she'd prefer to deal with this in private and not in public. I suggested that she acknowledge his anger.

Practice 2

Boss delivers diatribe, Priti opens her mouth but again is silent.

Priti's learning 2

It really is very hard to interrupt a torrent. Priti had to practise a few times increasing the volume of her own voice to match the volume of his and also to use his name to get his attention.

Practice 3

Boss delivers diatribe.

Priti   (interrupting in a firm tone of voice): 'Peter.'
Boss continues.
Priti   (in a louder voice): 'Peter! (he hesitates) I'm shocked at you bursting in like this.' (Maintaining eye contact with him) I can see you're angry but I would prefer to talk about this privately.'
Peter   (brandishing a document, but speaking more quietly): 'What is your explanation for this?'
Priti: 'I'd like to talk to you about this privately. Shall I come to your office in 10 minutes?'
Peter grunts in agreement but leaves the office.

Priti's learning 3

Priti was amazed that it was actually possible to begin to handle the situation, as she had previously felt far too frightened. Feeling intimidated by the actuality or possibility of other people's aggression has a detrimental effect on our self-esteem in the long term. The more we fear, the less space we take up psychologically. Once we can begin to expand into our own space and experience our own boundaries more firmly, we begin to feel our own feet on the ground physically and psychologically. It gradually becomes easier to respond with self-disclosure because this is coming from within ourselves and allowing us to set limits of many different kinds with clarity, even when faced with other people's outright aggression and hostility.

This approach is clearly in marked contrast to hoarding small pebbles of grievance and resentment and a sense of failure. Next, we look at how our experience of criticism and put-downs affects our image of ourselves.

eight

Managing criticism

The stereotypical accusation that a woman cannot handle criticism (like a man) and tends to take it too personally has a certain amount of truth in it. This is not to say that men are better at either giving or receiving criticism but, for many women, the ability to respond to criticism without being wounded is easily undermined by our need for approval.

If you look again at the diagram in Chapter 6 and recall how much we depend on *others* – their thoughts, opinions, love, blessings and permission – around which we construct our sense of personal identity, it is easy to understand why the experience of criticism is so close to rejection. Most of us do anything and everything to avoid falling short, being found to be inadequate or wrong or at fault: in fact being criticized in any way at all.

This part of the course takes a look at how to manage criticism assertively, which in turn gives an invaluable insight into how to pass on critical comments to others. Managing criticism is another aspect of establishing a personal boundary and seeing it as a two-way process, not just as an attack. Do I agree with it, if it is true? How do I contradict it, if untrue? How do I sort out a mixed criticism and agree with part of it if it is partly true while not accepting the whole comment?

The first and huge stumbling block comes from our past experience of criticism. We usually experienced criticism as unpleasant, and delivered from one in a position of power (parent, teacher or other adult). If we believed the criticism to be unfair and untrue and decided to contradict the adult in question, it was likely that we ended up with more criticism. If it was true and accompanied by punishment – disapproval, withdrawal of privileges, treats or physical punishment – we learnt that to be criticized was bad and equated it with *rejection*.

We carry also from the past an experience of *labels*. Most criticism comes in the form of a label or generalization: 'You're stupid/incompetent/clumsy/disorganized.' These labels stick to you as a *person*, not to your behaviour. Many women remember labels from their past that still exercise a powerful effect on them. Even if no one actually uses them anymore, unconsciously we allow words or phrases like fat, unmusical, too clever, nice, clumsy, slow, 'full of yourself', brainy (not pretty like your sister), to shape our behaviour and expectations of ourselves as adults.

Three familiar and usual approaches to criticism in all kinds of relationships, including working relationships, are the following:

- *Aggressive* (using boxing gloves). A defensive strategy aimed at disproving the criticism and attacking the accuser in turn.
- *Indirectly aggressive* (putting the boot in). This response is more covert. Nothing may be said at the time but the criticism stings and feels like an accusation: it will never be forgotten. At some point in time – and it may be a very long time – it will be used against the accuser in order to gain some revenge.
- *Passive* (grovelling). This strategy is again focused on accusation and punishment but this time the target is oneself. If someone, for example, points out a small error in an otherwise excellent report, the grovelling approach would go something like this: 'I don't know why I bother to do these things. I've never been any good at spelling. I might as well redo the whole report or, better still, get someone else to do it who *is* competent and can spell; in fact they might as well have my job...'

You may recognize one familiar response to criticism or see yourself in all three approaches at different times with different people. None of these responses actually entails *listening* to what is said, so this is the first stage in managing criticism:

- Listen to what the person is saying to you, or trying to say even if clumsily.
- Consider then: is it true? If the answer is yes, then how do you feel about it? You might accept it as part of your character or as a chronic habit. An example might be leaving things to the last minute, which works well for you even though it might be a cause for criticism in someone else's eyes. On the other hand, a tendency to be domineering may also be true but recognizing it may cause discomfort. It is important to notice what you feel about the criticism because self-disclosure is part of management.
- If you listen to the other person and the criticism strikes you as *un*true, it is important to disagree with the criticism. This takes confidence to do but it is as necessary to disagree with inappropriate criticism, as it is to acknowledge it when it is true.
- Sometimes we are criticized in a way that is partly true but not entirely. Whenever the words 'always' or 'never' are used, it is hard to accept that sometimes we can be aggressive, make a mistake or behave insensitively when part of us rightly wants to reject the generalization. This category of criticism calls for learning to agree and disagree at the same time.

If your usual approach is closer to the boxing glove, it is important to learn to listen. If the criticism is true, you can acknowledge it is true and if you use self-disclosure you will be able to avoid being defensive. This is the hardest task: to avoid the knee-jerk response of aggression and its counterpart, the position of apology and self-abasement.

Self-disclosure is the key. We tend to avoid it in this kind of situation and it is helpful to practise acknowledging criticism that may have a lingering sting from past experience. Sometimes we get sick and tired of hearing the same old thing, or associate a criticism with unfairness because we felt that we could do nothing about it, or it may be really hurtful. Whatever your feelings, heed your internal response and communicate it. This will help avoid either of the two extremes of aggression or apology.

A more surprising aspect of working on criticism is not only how we agree with true criticism, but also how difficult it is to disagree when we really believe that something is untrue or unfair. I relate this back to our inadequately established boundaries. When we depend so much on others for our self-definition, we lose sight over the years of what does and does not constitute the self that we recognize. This results in taking on board criticism that does not fit: simply because someone else has criticized us is enough to shake the fragile security of our own convictions.

Clearly, as individuals, we do not live in a vacuum, and other people's perceptions and comments, precisely because they come from outside us, can be illuminating and helpful. This, after all, is the fundamental purpose of human interaction, to exchange ideas and perceptions and learn from them. I know how much I value the perceptions of close friends who often challenge and surprise me and make me reassess my own assumptions.

But this depends on there being an exchange. If we simply take on board everything that everyone says to us, without consideration or contesting it, if untrue, we lose sight of who we are in the confusion. This is why it is crucial to learn the skill of disagreeing with criticism when appropriate. Disagreement does not have to be in the form of a battle. An assertive response does not mean having to win: it means very clearly stating that you disagree while at the same time leaving the door open for the other person to explain more fully what they mean.

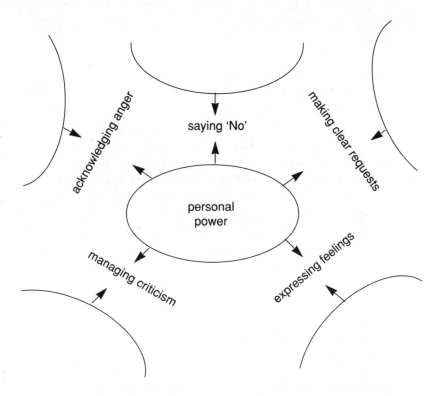

Figure 8.1

Practising an assertive response helps you to be more flexible. Does this criticism fit with your experience of yourself? Does it surprise you? Hurt you? Worry you? Consider the following examples:

Tracy is told by her boss, in the course of her annual appraisal, that she needs to be more committed. This word strikes a note of surprise and confusion. Below are four possible ways of responding to what she considers an unfair criticism:

- *Aggressive (tone of voice and body language defensive, feeling tearful and furious at the same time).* 'I think that's really unfair. I'm more committed than most of the others in the team. I don't know where you get that idea from.'
- *Indirectly aggressive.* She keeps quiet, seething inside, holding it as a grievance. This is unlikely to be directly expressed to her boss but she won't forget the comment. It will probably be hoarded among other grievances, and is likely to undermine her real commitment in some way.
- *Passive.* She again keeps quiet. The word 'uncommitted' hangs over her for days and, even though it feels unjust, she allows the criticism to go round and round in her head. She argues with herself but ends up convinced that, despite her own contradictory perception, the criticism must have some truth in it.
- *Assertive.* Tracy is direct. 'I'm very surprised that you say that, Jim. In fact, I'm quite shocked (*self-disclosure*) because, to my mind, I'm extremely committed to my work and to the team (*disagreement and contradiction*). Can you be more specific, because I don't understand.' (*Leaving the door open to the critic to be clearer.*)

Now compare the four possible responses in the next dialogue.

Jenny is walking down the corridor with a colleague after a meeting in which she had voiced a request to give a certain employee, who was under review, another chance.

Bill: 'You're too soft, Jenny. This is a tough world, you know, you can't keep living in fairyland.'

Jenny feels defensive, irritated and attacked by his put-down.

She can respond in the following ways:

- *Aggressive.* 'I *don't* live in fairyland. Why do you always have to dismiss my views as naïve? I suppose you think I am not tough enough to be professional. Is that it?'
- *Indirectly aggressive.* (*She mutters quietly.*) 'A little more concern about others wouldn't go amiss in this organization.'
- *Passive.* She responds with silence. She worries about his comment, which increases her self-doubt as to whether she really is too naïve and soft. This undermines her confidence.
- *Assertive.* 'Bill, I get so frustrated (*self-disclosure*) when you dismiss what I say like that; I am not soft. Of course I believe in a firm structure... we just have different values, that's all. I believe in caring for an individual as a person as well as an object in the organization. What do you mean exactly when you dismiss my behaviour as too soft?' (*Leaves door open for further exchange.*)

Expressing what you feel and yet still making it possible for the other person to clarify or be more specific leaves you able to establish your own boundary without being defensive. Many women argue that they are able to take a criticism if it is done in a nice way, if it is given constructively. In my experience, most men and women, in and out of the workplace, do not give criticism constructively, so beginning to build a more secure inner base from which to handle criticism, however, whenever and from whomever it comes, is the beginning of true confidence.

Once you build more confidence, you will be able to ask for criticism instead of waiting for it. This applies to situations even where you have an annual appraisal. Instead of waiting for the year to go round, consider making an appointment with your supervisor or line manager and ask for feedback, both positive and negative, on how you are doing. This also applies to those situations where you spend an inordinate amount of time fretting, worrying, and being preoccupied by what you fear somebody is thinking about you. Is he satisfied with my performance? Do they think I am doing a good job? Was she irritated by my suggestion? Did he feel put down by my comment? Do they think I ought to be more authoritative?

These and similar questions go round and round in our heads, consuming an awful lot of time and energy. Setting the scene – making the time to ask *directly* the person or people concerned – encourages them in turn to feel confident about being able to be direct with you.

One of the problems with responding to criticism is that it is often implicit rather than explicit. This refers to those veiled comments, innuendoes, pauses, gestures, mannerisms, or facial expressions that communicate criticism even if you are not quite sure what it is.

Responding in these situations is different, but the starting point (self-disclosure) is the same: what do you feel in response to the comment or gesture? Voicing your feeling, without accusation, is the most effective way of holding your own ground. Never mind whether you have a sense of humour, whether or not you are imagining the criticism when there isn't one, whether you are right or wrong. Managing such experiences starts with your own response: if you keep your feet on the ground psychologically, you can ask for more clarity or for an end to the behaviour if it is offensive or unkind, as in the following example.

Karen, originally from Germany, had lived and worked in England for 12 years. In a meeting, after she had voiced a proposal for a certain plan of action, a colleague piped up, with a mocking German accent: 'Vee haf vays of making you talk.'

At the time, she said nothing. One racist comment like this can tap into a vast reservoir of feeling from individual and collective experience. How could she respond without becoming bogged down in it all?

Practice 1

Colleague makes comment...
   Her response was the same as before, a shocked and embarrassed silence.

Karen's learning 1

What did she feel about the comment, I asked. 'Angry and unbelieving,' she said, 'I was completely shocked.' This was a good beginning.

Practice 2

Colleague makes comment...

Karen: 'I don't believe you said that... I feel quite shocked and very angry.'

An air of awkwardness hangs over the group.

Karen's learning 2

The whole issue of racism in all its forms is big, very big, so how do you begin to address it? Basically, in this public situation, you can't. The best way for everyone concerned is to close the dialogue and move on. More detailed discussion about the issues of racism can be handled away from a public arena, in which the only possible outcome is one winner and one loser.

Practice 3

Colleague makes comment...

Karen, looking directly at the speaker: 'I am quite shocked, John, and hurt by that.' (*Looking away from him to the rest of the group and changing her tone of voice):* 'I made a proposal and I wondered if any of you agree with my suggestion?'

After a few practices, Karen was able to handle this comment with great authority and dignity, meriting a lot of applause from us all.

Karen's learning 3

Karen was surprised that she could feel so many sensations in her body and how they changed as she became more confident in handling the situation. If you're wondering why it is relevant to practise handling a situation once it is in the past and unlikely to be repeated, remember the function of role-play. When role-play is properly used, your whole psychosomatic system is involved: you are not just talking about the issue, but feeling the feelings physically as well. This allows a new learning to take place, in the mind and body simultaneously.

When we fail to deal with the situation, the memory of the experience stays locked in our minds and bodies, reinforced every time something similar occurs. These images and associations remain part of our lives, in the body/mind memory. In a similar situation, our thoughts are affected by perceptions of failure, inadequacy, powerlessness, and so on, making it extra hard to behave differently in the face of accumulated feelings.

When we practise handling ourselves assertively, in a role-play, we re-establish an alternative perception, an alternative association in the body/mind memory. This alternative allows for a recognition and management of the anxiety and other emotions instead of being overcome by them. Slowly, each time we do this, our body/mind is able to build an alternative image that offers a picture of 'I can' instead of 'I can't'.

nine

Handling authority

The process described in the next two chapters looks at how we offer criticism to others. This is sometimes called 'confrontation', making it very clear how aggressive we expect the experience to be. At other times, offering criticism is called 'feedback', more restrained and official perhaps, but this can still be aggressive and insensitive in intention and experience.

The skills relevant to giving criticism – at work, at home, at play – are relevant whenever we want to ask for someone to improve, correct or change their behaviour. They can be seen most simply as informing someone when their behaviour conflicts with your expectations, needs and wishes. So why is the prevailing image of confrontation a weapon? Why, if we decide to confront someone, do we anticipate defeat or victory and prepare to do battle accordingly?

Our anxieties about confrontation fall into one of two categories, which will reflect whether we perceive ourselves as potentially the winner or the loser in this battle. If we happen to see ourselves as having the *greater* power, we find ourselves making the following rationalizations:

'She's going through a rough time at the moment.'

'He'd be devastated if I'd said anything.'

'I don't want to appear too authoritarian.'

'We all have our little faults, don't we?'

'He doesn't know he's doing it. Bless...'

'She means well...'

'I feel sorry for him really.'

If, in relation to the individual concerned, we identify ourselves as having *less* power and potentially being the loser, a different set of rationalizations emerge:

'There's no point in bothering.'

'It won't make any difference.'

'It will end up in a nasty mess.'

'He won't listen to me.'

'They will have even more power over me.'

'She'll always hold it against me.'

Winning and losing dominate our conscious (and unconscious) thoughts because aggression has become so deeply ingrained in us.

When I introduce the idea of equality in the course, it is met with a certain amount of incredulity. How can we be equal when power is distributed so unevenly in life?

Conflicts between 'them up there' and 'them down here' are constantly facing us at work and elsewhere: there are those who have power and those who don't. This is true, but only in relation to *one* kind of power.

Hierarchical power, like a ladder, only offers the possibility of travelling up or down. I call this perpendicular power. It comes from an external source and comes attached to various 'commodities' with which we may be born or which we acquire in the course of our lives.

External sources of power

One example of external power is resources. Resources include money, education, information, land; being articulate, numerate, literate; having access to other individuals with external power. All of us experience having this kind of power over others at some time in our lives: we have more money than some and less than others, we have more education and information than some and less than others. The more/less measurement means that those with resources have power over those who have fewer or none.

A second example is societal power that is granted in a ranking system, those higher up having power over those below. A parent has power over a child, a teacher over a pupil, a manager over a department, a director over several managers, a mayor over a council, an emperor over an empire, and so on. The nature of power here is one of position, role and status which carries with it legitimate power. Once again, all of us, at different times in the hierarchical world in which we live and work, experience being over some and under others at the same time.

A third example of external power is expertise. This relates to the power that comes from ability, skill, talent, training and education. Expertise in any field means that you have power over others with less or no expertise: you will also experience the reverse in some aspects of your life, where you are vulnerable precisely because you have to depend on someone else for the expertise you don't have.

A final example of external power is referent power. This describes the less concrete but no less powerful commodity of appeal that can come in the form of sex appeal and attractiveness. It is described as charisma, charm, magnetism and persuasiveness. It is the kind of power that people respond to by imitating, obeying, following, moulding themselves upon, even parting with their money and sanity along the way. It is evident in the imitation and adulation of sports or pop stars and seen in a variety of ways in which we look up to and try to model ourselves on someone else as an ideal.

We are usually only conscious of this perpendicular form of power when interacting with other people. Because we are so preoccupied with this one form, it comes as a surprise to consider the parallel existence of a second kind of power. This is quite different, more nebulous in nature and less easy to describe. Nevertheless, it is real, tangible and noticeable both in its absence and presence. Here, power is *internal*, coming from a source within our being. Aspects of it include:

- Freedom to be oneself.
- Self-esteem.
- Spontaneity.
- Integrity.
- Self-trust.
- Emotional attunement.
- Wisdom (as distinct from knowledge).
- Flexibility.
- Awareness of boundaries.
- Self-realization.

The first major difference is that internal power is an abiding power. It can be seen in unsophisticated form in small children. It develops, if encouraged, into adulthood and can last a lifetime. By contrast, sources of external power are temporary. Resources are limited and finite; expertise only carries power when that particular skill is needed by others: family, professional and social roles and status change along with the power that accompanies them; attractiveness to others, measured by the prevailing cultural norm, is temporary. We find ourselves sometimes with power over others and at other times we find ourselves without it.

The qualities of personal power, on the other hand, are not commodities, which means they cannot be bought, sold or bartered in the same way as aspects of external power. Yet although personal power comes from within and does not depend upon the same sources as external power, it still fluctuates. It waxes and wanes according to life experiences, as a child, as an adult, at home, at work, in society at large. The kinds of life experience that account for the lowering of personal power include:

Constant criticism

Ignorance of alternative strategies

Isolation and lack of support

Over-protection

Unexpressed feelings

A constant intimation of inadequacy

No access to learning alternatives

Depression

Avoidance

Fatigue/illness

Fear of reprisals

Denial

Managing internal and external power is a challenge. Some of us are more comfortable with external power than others. Distinguishing between the two is essential because there are times when we have external power but feel internally powerless, and times when we are defeated by the system but retain our personal power.

There is nothing inherently wrong with power over others. It comes as part and parcel of the structure of the world in which we live. Our difficulties arise in the way that we choose to use or abuse this power over others. If used aggressively, external power becomes oppression.

How do we oppress others? There are obvious examples of institutional and social oppression using gender (sexism), nationality/culture/colour of skin (racism), sexual preferences (heterosexism), age (ageism) as an excuse or rationalization for all kinds of oppressive behaviour. These range from exclusion and disregard, through victimization and bullying to extreme abuse and extermination. Most of us will have suffered, in some way, as a result of these forms of institutional oppression.

Even in our ordinary lives, we are capable of oppressing others, often unaware that we are doing so. The following examples apply in both personal and professional contexts:

☐ Keeping someone over-dependent.

☐ Making choices and decisions for others inappropriately. Obviously some choices have to be made for others without consultation, but it is also used as a strategy to gain or retain external power over other people.

☐ Exercising legitimate power but not allowing the other person to express their feelings in response to your actions or decisions. This is a common example of oppressive behaviour between employer and employee, and between parents and children.

☐ Maintaining a tight control in personal relationships.

☐ Failing to confront prejudiced assumptions about oneself and others.

☐ Excluding others from participation. Again this is sometimes necessary but it leaves a wide margin open to abuse because of the need to hold on to external power.

Handling authority as women

How do we manage to be authoritative without being authoritarian? How can we carry out the role and responsibilities of our legitimate power without this degenerating into oppression?

I don't believe that men handle this conflict any more effectively than women, but most men feel more at home with the aggressive, competitive model because of conditioning. I find that many women instinctively move towards a sense of concern for the other person and try to balance this with their authority... and then hesitate.

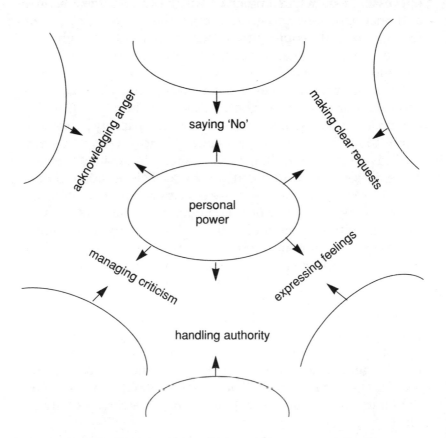

Figure 9.1

The concern to avoid being oppressive is one aspect of our hesitation. We do not always feel comfortable 'pulling rank' because we do not want to threaten the other individual's sense of equal participation and inclusion. We do not want to alienate others in this way and jeopardize the possibility of cooperation. Looking more carefully at what constitutes oppression can help. In other words, we can learn to handle authority assertively, to give others a chance to express their feelings, to treat people with respect even if they are below us in the hierarchy. These principles help to avoid oppressive behaviour.

The other aspect of hesitation is more deeply rooted in us and is harder to address. The weakness in handling authority for most women stems from our fear of visibility. Although our need for approval – for being liked or loved – extends into our private lives as well, many of us remain hostage to a fear of being seen or 'found out' at work. This is not rational, because fear often isn't; yet it exercises a powerful hold on our thinking and behaviour. Thoughts run along the lines of: 'If I stand out, they might see through me; I might be wrong, then they'll see I'm an imposter, then they'll attack me.' This is connected to a need to feel fully confident and absolutely sure so that we can cope with any response. We have to know we are *right* and in full control.

In an organization that allows no room for fallibility or honesty (which is the norm), the well-known phenomenon of 'bullshitting' will automatically appear as a response to the fear of getting it wrong. When this is the prevailing and accepted strategy, I find that women tend to avoid doing the same, but instead resort to a secondary strategy of invisibility.

Our response to these anxieties tends to be aggressive or passive. If we're anxious about what someone else will think, it is an easy step to do as others do: be abrupt, arrogant, intimidating, show you mean business, look tough and be as hard as nails. It is important never to lose sight of the fact that this behaviour stems from *anxiety*, not true confidence or a sense of personal power.

When we don't want to behave in this aggressive manner, we tend towards a less visible option. We speak too softly, unsteadily, lacking in firmness and clarity. We are vague instead of specific; we fail to take ourselves seriously and are insufficiently direct in our approach.

The balance is in managing authority assertively. This is part of setting limits. We have looked at the importance of personal boundaries for ourselves. In the workplace we may need to express our own boundaries as well as those of the organization.

Tessa wanted to confront a member of her team, a man who was popular and a good salesman but who would never get his end-of-month figures to her on time. She had asked several times before but with no success.

As we discussed her situation, Tessa admitted that she was insecure about asking because she felt a little undermined by him and had the impression that he wasn't really taking her seriously as his manager. This both irritated and worried her.

I suggested she took the initiative and set the scene. This was difficult to arrange because he was hardly ever in the office, so she decided to rehearse the following telephone call.

Practice 1

Tessa: 'Hello Bob.'

Bob: 'Hi.'

Tessa: 'Look, I am phoning about the figures again. You're a week late and I've got everyone else's in. Any chance you can get them to me?'

Bob: 'I am sorry, Tessa, I will get them done when I can... but I just haven't had a moment.'

Tessa's learning 1

Her response was that this was how he always replied, but he would never deliver. In our discussion she realized that it was a pattern now and she would do better to meet him face to face. She knew he'd be in the office for a team meeting so decided to ask him to meet her for 10 minutes before the meeting.

Practice 2

Tessa: 'Hello, Bob. Take a seat… thanks for coming.'
Bob *(defensively):* 'This is all a bit formal, isn't it?'
Tessa: 'Well, it is a little formal but it's important.'
Bob: 'So what have I done wrong now?' *(in the tone of a schoolboy talking to a teacher)*
Tessa: 'Well, it's not… you haven't done anything wrong, it's just that…' She stopped.

Tessa's learning 2

Tessa felt she had started off on the wrong foot and had become defensive. She asked to start again. Recognizing when you've 'lost it', so to speak, and correcting yourself marks an important transition precisely because the recognition comes from within instead of in response to an external prompt. This is what helps to transfer the skills to real life.

Practice 3

Tessa: 'Hello, Bob. Take a seat … thanks for coming.'
Bob: 'What's with the formal meeting then?'
Tessa *(not getting hooked by Bob's manner but staying with her own power):* 'I don't find this easy, Bob, but the situation now is serious. Each month I chase you for your returns, and each month you are late. This means I send them late to the head office. I'd like to have them in on time.'
Bob: 'So what does it matter if they're a bit late? My figures are good and that's what matters, not the admin.'
Tessa: 'I know your figures are good, but I still have to provide end-of-month team figures, whether I want to or not, and I need yours on time, Bob. Do you understand?'
Bob *(a little mockingly):* 'Yes, Miss.'
Tessa: 'You don't have to take that attitude, Bob.'

She looked at me and said this was exactly how he'd behave.

Tessa's learning 3

Does it *matter*? Does it matter if she behaves assertively and clearly and does her job with authority, that Bob feels compelled to respond with sarcasm or mockery?

If the answer is 'Yes', you have a very arduous task ahead trying to smooth everything out, please everyone, keep them smiling and ensure a happy ending for all.

If the answer is 'No', you can shelve your need to be liked. You can accept that many men of all ages have difficulty with women in positions of authority and are likely to project all sorts of stereotypes onto you. You may be subjected to these from women employees as well.

The route you take will depend on your own boundary and your own personal power, which is why so much of this book is about setting limits. With a firm boundary and an awareness of personal power, you will be able to shrug your shoulders when this happens even though it can be irritating, infuriating and sometimes extremely hurtful. It will and does happen a lot.

Practice 4

Tessa: 'Hello, Bob. Take a seat ... thanks for coming.'

Bob: 'What's with the formal meeting then?'

Tessa *(not getting hooked by Bob's manner but staying with her own power):* 'I don't find this easy, Bob, but the situation now is serious. Each month I chase you for your returns, and each month you are late. This means I send them late to head office. I'd like to have them in on time.'

Bob: 'So what does it matter if they're a bit late? My figures are good and that's what matters, not the admin.'

Tessa: 'I know your figures are good, but I still have to provide end-of-month team figures, whether I want

	to or not, and I need yours on time, Bob, do you understand?'
Bob	*(a little mockingly):* 'Yes, Miss.'
Tessa,	*taking a deep breath (anxious inside but with more external assurance):* 'I don't find this easy, Bob, but I'd like your figures by the end of the month, and I'd like your agreement to this. This is not a personal favour: it's for everyone else's benefit as well.'
Bob	*(with a loud sigh):* 'Well, I'll see what I can do.'
Tessa	*(getting into her stride now):* 'I need those figures on time, Bob.'
Bob:	'Okay.' *(Getting up.)*
Tessa:	'Thanks for coming.'

Tessa's learning 4

Tessa was shaking but less from anxiety than conviction. 'It's true,' she said. 'It isn't personal... and it really doesn't matter.'

A working relationship is bounded by considerations of work, not friendships or intimacy. Reminding yourself of this boundary is a great help. It doesn't mean that you have to be unfeeling, heartless or robotic. You can still be human, even when you are operating in a professional and authoritative manner.

ten

Giving criticism effectively

Giving criticism hinges on a sense of equality with the other person, so a simultaneous awareness of the two aspects of power – hierarchical *and* personal – is crucial when learning how to give criticism. The picture changes from one in which you are trying to establish yourself as right rather than wrong or as winner instead of loser, into one in which you want to address a particular situation because it matters to you in some way. You want to stop being power-less or giving your personal power away but without needing to impose your will or opinions or emotions in steamroller-like fashion. We can begin to see this process – both in a work and a personal context – as one that involves a measure of care or at least respect for the other person as well as oneself; in other words, seeing the other person as an equal human being.

I'm aware, while writing this, how frequently I emphasize equality. This is because we have become so accustomed to interacting with others on an up/down basis, that a genuine understanding of the implications requires us to make a shift of consciousness.

The main thing to remember is that the key lies within our attitude. It doesn't matter whether you are 'entitled' to correct someone, whether you have the authority to draw a line or to issue an ultimatum, in other words whether or not you have hierarchical power over someone else, because the following process is rooted in a fundamental approach of equality. You do not need to assemble the ammunition beforehand or to build a cast-iron case: this always predetermines an approach of aggression. You do, however, need to be clear about what you feel and what you want.

When do we need to confront?

The skills apply when we want to express what we feel about past behaviour and how we would like to be treated differently in the future. They apply when we are addressing a habit, a tendency, a manner in someone that annoys, hurts or intimidates us. They apply when we need to terminate a contract or when we need to challenge what is happening to us personally, or to our department or team. These skills involve maintaining a balance between equality and hierarchy, when we challenge and confront what we experience as unacceptable, unfair, inadequate, hurtful, insensitive, wasteful or bullying behaviour in others.

Above all, these skills apply when there is a history: when what you are addressing has happened more than once, when it is happening repeatedly so that you are challenging a pattern in someone's behaviour and a pattern in your own response to it.

When we begin a course by asking for examples of real-life situations which participants would like to manage more effectively, many of the situations described have a history. This refers to the problems in our lives that resemble a large and daunting pile of stones. We look at the pile and feel uncertain and overwhelmed. It looks big, it feels complicated and is certainly emotionally charged. It has become big, complicated and emotionally charged because of its history, made up of each single stone, each single incident, recorded, remembered and often misperceived.

The combination of the effects of the passage of time, the number of interwoven incidents and the unexpressed feelings add up to an emotionally fraught situation. So how can we begin?

First, we learn to use the skills in less difficult situations so that we become familiar with them, rather like learning to drive a simple engine before negotiating a more powerful and complex one.

The other reason for leaving these heavyweight situations until later in the course is that, as the distinction between aggression and assertiveness becomes clearer, we will have begun to understand that nobody else can be 100 per cent to blame for our behaviour. Accepting partial responsibility because of previous lack of clear communication will help to put aside the need to punish and avenge ourselves. Genuinely letting go of this need will automatically make it easier for the other person to listen because they won't have to defend themselves from your attack.

Choosing one stone from the pile helps to side-step self-defeating messages: 'There's no point/I can't do anything about it/it's impossible.' It changes to an awareness that you can do something, however small it may appear in relation to the rest of the pile. Making this first move also tells you that the other person and the situation are important to you in some way, important enough for you to take the time and trouble to sort things out between you.

The following stages describe the best way to proceed, if you want to achieve a constructive outcome.

● Set the scene.

We have already described the importance of doing this. It is especially important when wanting to challenge a pattern of behaviour. It feels formal and it *is* formal: trying to pretend it's a casual matter is a waste of time because if it *were* casual and trivial you wouldn't be having this difficulty with it. This applies even in a relationship that is personal. Setting aside the time to speak with your colleague, employee, boss, friend, parent or partner is the first step. This may be a formal appointment or saying to someone closer that you have to talk about something important to you, distinguishing this from an ordinary day-to-day exchange.

Before you start, be clear about what it is you want to change. What exactly is it that the other person does or fails to do that is the issue? Don't aim for a total personality remould: you need to be specific. Then consider how you feel about this behaviour, not what you think, but how you feel. Then decide what you would like instead. If you can't decide what you actually want, *don't begin*.

Once you have the answers to these three questions and have set the scene, you can proceed.

● Use self-disclosure.

One of the mistakes we make early on is denying our anxiety. If you don't use self-disclosure, your tone and body language will be aggressive or passive. A simple but true statement such as 'This is hard for me' or 'I feel awkward bringing this up' will suffice.

● Specify the behaviour.

Be clear and precise about the other person's behaviour:

'When you turn up late for work...'

'When you shout at me in front of everyone...'

'When you don't balance the books...'

'When you don't give me any feedback...'

● Express what you feel.

'I feel...

... frustrated.'

... embarrassed.'

... irritated.'

... insecure.'

● Request the change you want.

'I would like you to...

... come in on time at 9 am.'

... speak to me in private if you want to criticize me.'

... go back over the figures and make them balance.'

... make the time for constructive criticism about my work.'

This completes the first part of the encounter, in other words, your statement. Now, in order to make this a two-way encounter, you need to invite the other person to respond.

● Be open to a response.

This can take the form of checking for understanding or seeking agreement with your request. For example:

'Do you have a problem getting here on time or can you ensure you are punctual in the future?'

'Can you agree to this?'

'Will you have any difficulty doing this?'

'Would you be willing to make the time?'

● Repeat and clarify.

Depending on the response, you may need to repeat your request, emphasize your own feelings or clarify your request for change. If the other person needs time to think about a response, make sure you have a time arranged before you part company.

Sometimes, it is helpful to end with a statement such as:

'Thanks for coming to talk about this.'

'I'd appreciate your agreement with this.'

'Things will run more efficiently if you do this.'

'I'm pleased to have been able to talk to you.'

It can also mean inviting the other person to express any feelings they have in response. This is especially relevant in personal relationships, where, what being aware of it, we risk being oppressive when we exercise legitimate power appropriately, but prevent someone expressing their emotional response to our actions.

In the workplace, this 'hit and run' approach is the norm both at an organizational and a one-to-one level. It is usually related to an inability to deal with anyone's feelings and a reluctance to take responsibility for the fact that what you have had to implement in the course of your work will cause hurt or anger in someone else. Terminating employment, for example, is often an occasion for such abuse. Instead of an employee discovering his or her dismissal by arriving at work on Monday to find someone else at his or her desk, the use of appropriate skills would enable the employer to treat the employee with respect.

● Close the conversation.

The final stage of this procedure is closure. Since you have initiated the encounter, you must close it. This can mean simply changing the subject or standing up and seeing the person out of the room, leaving the room yourself, putting down the telephone, ending the conversation in some way. This is because you had to make it formal to start with and you need therefore to end it formally.

You need to do this for both of you. Even if you have

managed it well, you may feel awkward at the end and the other person is quite likely to feel 'told off 'or surprised, so it is a relief for both parties to bring the encounter to an end and to get on with something else.

Whenever we want to tackle a situation with a history (in other words, when a pattern of behaviour has been established that you want to challenge or correct), it is important to use the steps described above *beforehand* in order to be clear about what you want to achieve. This will be your starting point.

Wendy, a supervisor in a large canteen, wanted to criticize one of the young women employed there as a cook. The woman concerned was habitually late and Wendy also felt she had an 'attitude' problem: she didn't show much enthusiasm for anything and worked in a half-hearted way most of the time. Wendy worked out two specific aspects of the behaviour: arriving late and not showing any enthusiasm. The specific change she wanted was easier to identify for the first aspect: she wanted her to arrive on time, at 8.30 am like everyone else.

The second aspect was not so clear, except a vague wish for more enthusiasm. This is not specific enough and it tells us that instead of making a specific request, it is more appropriate to open a dialogue. This is because you cannot proceed without more information: Why is the employee unenthusiastic ... what's going on at work or at home that contributes to this ... is there anything that Wendy herself could do differently to change the situation, and so on?

Wendy identified her feelings as irritation at the lateness and concern about the apparent lack of willingness to work. Wendy's practice went something like this.

Practice 1

Wendy has set the scene by asking Alice to come and see her in her office.

Wendy: 'Hello, Alice, take a seat (*said with an over-bright smile*). I just wanted to have a little chat to find out how things were going... are you happy here, do you think?'

Alice (*edgy, defensive*): 'What do you mean, am I happy here?'

Wendy's learning 1

It's so tempting to use some *nice*, friendly but ultimately misleading preamble. This is a common way to dissipate anxiety ... our own. However, it is extremely unhelpful, because the other person becomes more tense and defensive, knowing that something is coming and wondering when. Our own anxiety increases as well. It is better to come to the point as soon as possible.

Practice 2

Wendy: 'Hello, Alice, take a seat... Look, I don't find this sort of thing easy but it's part of my job as your supervisor. I've noticed you come frequently late to work and I'm frustrated because I have to get everyone started at work. I'd like you to come at 8.30 like everyone else. Also, you don't show much enthusiasm for your work so I wanted to have a chat with you and find out if there is anything wrong. Is there any reason why you come late?'

Alice needs to know clearly that she has to arrive on time, but the question at the end allows her to tell Wendy if there is a problem that can then be discussed.

Wendy's learning 2

Wendy learnt from the feedback that this way of handling the beginning of a dialogue leaves the other person open and able to respond, instead of feeling threatened and defensive. It is important to specify the change when you can, but also be able to gather relevant information when this is more appropriate.

When a criticism falls into the second category, it is still important to specify your request, but in the light of information from the other person. This quality of interaction offers the possibility of an exchange and takes it out of the traditional scenario of being 'told off' by someone in authority. It is often helpful to enquire whether the other person has anything to ask of *you*: whether you could behave differently or more supportively. This quality encourages the kind of honest interaction that is essential for committed teamwork.

Sometimes we need to confront somebody even when it's not officially our job to do so. Mary worked in a finance department and it was her colleague's task to balance the books each month. For the past six months, the figures had been wrong, and rather than say anything, Mary had taken to doing the work herself. How could she approach this more directly?

The specific behaviour in question was clearly the failure to get a proper balance and the change she wanted was to ensure a correct one. What were her feelings? Frustration and resentment accumulated after the past months of not saying anything before; also embarrassment because officially they were equals, and she found it hard to criticize an equal colleague.

Practice 1

She set the scene beforehand and arranged to meet in a quiet corner of the office.

Mary: 'Penny, I find this really awkward, but I'm really concerned about the balance sheets you've been doing. I end up doing them again and I don't think it's fair.'

Penny (taken aback, embarrassed): 'What do you mean, they're not correct?'

Mary: 'Well, they're not right. You don't do a proper balance, and I have to go over it myself!'

Penny   *(feeling unsure):* 'You mean last month's figures?'

Mary   *(exasperated tone):* 'No, it's been going on for at least six months!'

Penny   *(defensively):* 'So why haven't you said anything before?'

Mary: *Silenced.*

Mary's learning 1

It is crucial when using this process to take responsibility for *not* having spoken up in the past. The temptation is to blame the other person but it is in fact not Penny's fault that Mary said nothing earlier. This confusion and unwillingness to take responsibility adds the weight of blame to the specific request for change. This will always be experienced as an attack. As a consequence, the specific change that you want and that you have the right to ask for will be lost under the resentment. It is essential to separate what you want and what you feel about the specific behaviour from the backlog. Your pattern of response in the past is your responsibility alone. Don't waste time blaming yourself, just acknowledge it. Once you accept this, genuinely, you are much freer to make a specific request for change.

Practice 2

Mary: 'Penny, I'm feeling really anxious about bringing this up, which is why I haven't done so before. For the past few months the balance sheets have been wrong and I've had to do them again myself. Well, er, no... I didn't *have* to, I chose to because I didn't know what else to do. But now I'm getting upset about it all, well quite cross actually, and so I wanted to talk to you. I wanted to find out what's happening and what we can do about it.'

Mary's learning 2

Mary's feedback to herself this time was that she had been hesitant and anxious and fumbling with her words. The feedback to her, however, was that she had come across far more clearly and sympathetically, just by acknowledging responsibility for what she had done in the past instead of blaming Penny. Penny felt shocked, embarrassed, and awkward – all quite understandable feelings – but she didn't feel attacked.

It is important to remember that our words do not have to emerge with a slick articulacy. We are not delivering a script and if we hesitate and fumble occasionally for words this will not detract from the assertive spirit of the interaction. Being assertive is not about being polished. It means genuinely expressing your feelings and genuinely respecting the other person as an equal. It also includes being able to give praise when appropriate.

Giving compliments

Giving 'positive feedback' at an official review is different from spontaneous affirmation of a colleague, a subordinate or even a superior, which can be incorporated into everyday interaction. It doesn't mean being gushy, effusive or insincere, just appreciative.

The first challenge to address in giving appreciation is lack of specificity. Words like 'fantastic', 'brilliant', 'fabulous' slip very easily off the tongue and although they are certainly positive, it is worth making the extra effort if you want the feedback to be valuable. You need to go that bit further and specify what you feel and describe the other person's behaviour. This transforms...

- *a vague comment:* 'You were great with Derek' into 'I felt proud of the way you challenged Derek yesterday.'

- *a bland observation:* 'You'll do OK here' into 'I'm glad to have you on the team. You're a real asset.'
- *an understatement:* 'You're not bad considering...' into 'It's been a difficult job and you've done well. I'm very pleased.'
- *a near put-down:* 'You seem to be a lot more vocal lately' into 'You've been coming up with some good ideas recently. I'm impressed.'

... each a more meaningful token of esteem.

The main block we experience in this whole area is lack of familiarity with genuine affirmation. Few of us feel adequately valued for our efforts and this can breed a mean streak in us when it comes to openly valuing others. Yet, affirmation – simple, specific and sincere – when given in this way, is of equal importance to constructive criticism in creating a genuinely cooperative environment. This is why, apart from being a pleasure to do, it is an important aspect of handling authority effectively.

eleven

Gender at work – the more visible aspects

Whether you are working in a male-dominated environment, working in equal numbers, with women in the majority or in an all-female environment, gender issues affect us all, though we may not always be conscious of them. The following comments and questions reflect some of the more visible gender-related issues at work:

'In a male-dominated field, my ideas are dismissed.'

'I'm the only female lecturer in my department and would like to understand how this affects my position.'

'As a student I never felt treated differently from male colleagues. It is only since I started working that I feel the need to assert myself much more.'

'Why do men in the workplace still think that women should be supportive of them and not criticize them? How can one break this pattern?'

'I'm increasingly up against a very aggressive competitive male atmosphere: how do I cope?'

'Are we tolerated or accepted? As I increasingly find myself working with men, I feel the former is the case.'

'I realize that my office employs more women than men but the men hold all the senior positions. Why is this?'

'I'd like to become more confident in distinguishing between difficulties arising from my gender and difficulties arising out of my level of competence.'

'How can I survive in a largely male-dominated environment: should I learn to speak "male"?'

'How do I tackle male colleagues who are generally supportive and would be appalled at the thought of being sexist, yet are unaware of the, sometimes conspicuous, bias that informs their thinking?'

'I find it hard to deal with male aggression. I had to work for two years with a male manager whose temper drove many staff to tears, including me.'

'How do I deal with men in managerial positions who are apparently unwilling to accept the real responsibilities of managing? By this I mean developing and communicating a vision, leadership, setting priorities and commitment to the team.'

Several themes emerge here: intimidation by individual men, difficulty in confronting and challenging sexist attitudes and behaviour, a sense of having minority values, seeing mainly men in senior positions, sometimes inadequate to the task, and yet unchallenged.

Challenging a tradition

Women have always worked. We come from a tradition of centuries of domestic labour, paid and unpaid: a past and continuing tradition of exploitation of women and girls low down the economic scale, who are forced into powerless conditions of domestic servitude, prostitution, factory labour. Today there are legions of women higher up the economic scale, who lack skills and education or, having chosen to bring up their children, are then obliged to take whatever part-time piecemeal work they can. They have no security or status and therefore no power to combat exploitation from their employers. Women in the workplace are still, in historical terms, a novelty.

The pioneers who broke new ground towards the end of the nineteenth century and the early decades of the last one, paved the way for other women to receive the same educational and professional opportunities. Women have entered the workplace with the assurance of equal pay, equal status and equal opportunity: all very seductive, although the reality is often different. The women who are now in middle or senior administrative, commercial, academic, editorial, clinical or educational posts cannot claim the security of an established tradition behind them.

When any legislation is finally brought in after lengthy battles and tireless efforts by a few individuals who devote a great deal of their time and energy to changing conditions for the many, victory is proclaimed. However, legislation aimed to curb practices of racism or sexism will pre-date any change in the deep emotional response of individuals in society. Attitudes stem from profound and long-lasting beliefs, rooted in emotion and distorted perceptions, and will not be altered by the threat of sanction. As a particular ideology takes hold, comments that might previously have been acceptable, even endorsed in public, simply remain unspoken but are nevertheless *thought* and admitted in private. Hidden prejudice is, in many ways, far more insidious and more difficult to expose or challenge, precisely because it goes underground.

Change in a social system, within a given rank and hierarchy, occurs very slowly. Superficial change occurs more quickly but sexist attitudes, assumptions, stereotypes and inequities persist unchanged and untouched by the recommendations of law and policy makers. It is a nonsense to state that the experience of work is exactly the same whether you are male or female.

So how do these differences show themselves? First of all, it is easy to recognize different behaviour patterns and expectations. We can see different patterns of behaviour divided into four categories.

Visibility

Women are aware of being visible, of being looked *at*. Women are conscious of appearance, treading that very fine line between being seen as attractive and being seen as provocative in the way they are dressed. Women are aware of being rated: scoring top marks for being a young, attractive, high flier and low marks if you're middle aged and considered (in the culture) past the peak of desirability.

Women are often subject to comments on their dress and appearance and therefore will take care of how they will be *seen*.

Men, on the other hand, tend to conform to a uniform suit or more casual wear, depending on the context, but do not have the same experience of being constantly looked at. They tend to be more preoccupied with performance at work, physical attractiveness almost an irrelevance.

Touchability

Seeing women as objects is an attitude that dies hard because fantasy operates at a much deeper and more permanent level than conscious political correctness. Stereotypes persist. Estimating a woman's attractiveness is related to seeing a young girl in need of protection (daughter); this is related to seeing an older woman in need of patronage and tolerance (mother) and, in turn, is related to assuming permission to touch. This touch is not necessarily applied to the thigh or bottom (nothing so gross) but a shoulder, the face, an arm are still part of the same body and are often part of normal congress. The intent may not be sexual but the assumed permission to touch means that a woman's body, ie her own territory, is open to being touched without invitation. This is another compelling reason for women's difficulty in establishing their boundaries.

Touchability outside an intimate context is not reciprocal. Women do not feel the same permission to touch men's thighs or arms or faces. For the most part, this reflects a lack of interest in doing so, but there is also an assumption that if they did, it would be interpreted as explicitly sexual in intent. The combined experience of being constantly in view and liable to evaluation, as well as being touched without permission, is unlikely to generate feelings of confidence, relaxation, self-esteem or equality. A sense of powerlessness is inevitable.

Pleasability

The need to be attractive broadens out to the need to appear pleasing. This means smiling, looking interested, being calm, being supportive, obliging and attentive, speaking in a soft, muted tone of voice, being uncritical; generally behaving in a pleasant manner. Women lower their eyes more often when speaking and, as we find when practising in role-plays, we look away in deference.

On the other hand, men generally feel more permission to shout, to express anger, to glare, to stare and to intimidate. If they look away from someone it is more often intended as a dismissal, showing domination rather than submission.

Shrinkability

We shrink our bodies, quite literally, by taking up as little space as possible: we hunch our shoulders, we flinch, we lower our heads and stand lopsidedly. We rarely stand up straight and hold our ground: we tend to accommodate by adopting a yielding posture. We also shrink ourselves in our manner of speech: we hesitate, we over-apologize, we put ourselves down, we understate the importance of matters. We keep silent instead of raising points we want to raise; we don't challenge pretence; we don't challenge criticism. We hesitate to be clever, to be brilliant, to be outspoken; we don't dare. All these patterns of behaviour are part of this tendency to shrink.

Men, on the other hand, feel more permission to make authoritative and definitive pronouncements because they feel more genuinely at home in the culture. Men have the advantage of dealing with a system in which they are not newcomers. Physically, men often take up more space, which reflects a difference in size sometimes, but also a permission to assume more space. They often feel more comfortable with emphatic statements that discourage disagreement. Often they feel more at home with large desks and other executive *accoutrements* of hierarchical power.

The realization that there is a gender difference and that it is not in our imagination can help. This doesn't mean that we are always right. Sometimes we hear a put-down when there isn't one or wrongly attribute someone's criticism to a sexist attitude. Of course we make mistakes, but we can forgive ourselves and take responsibility knowing that reality is a lot more empowering than denial. The reality of sexism and racism in the workplace, as elsewhere in life, is undeniable. As part of that reality, many women experience harassment at work.

Sexual harassment

We tend to read of the more gross instances of sexual harassment in the press, but depending upon legislation to help us is costly and not necessarily reliable. The experience of a court case can be more harrowing for the victim than the offender and it is unlikely she will be able to stay in her job, even if she wants to, whether or not she 'wins'. Winning does not necessarily entail support, understanding, loyalty and respect. Frequently the victim – as with rape – is ostracized and even shamed for 'making such a fuss', 'dragging things through the court', 'causing everybody such a lot of embarrassment and harm'.

It is useful to place sexual harassment in a context of general harassment, in a context of the values that dominate not only in the workplace but also in the world at large. We can see harassment as part of an entire syndrome, consonant with attitudes to women, to women at work especially, in the conditioned responses of the majority of men, who would not dream of actually physically harassing a woman.

Feeling more permission to look at or touch a woman's body is embedded in the particular power structure in the world at large and therefore is not going to disappear, regardless of a commitment on paper to political correctness.

Seeing a sexist put-down as one part of a whole helps to put it into perspective. This, in turn, can also help us to deal with an individual man without launching into a tirade of blame for the whole experience of oppression. Role-play helps us to deal with one complaint instead of getting bogged down in the whole complex mess.

Geraldine wanted to know how she could have handled an incident with a former supervisor who, as she sat at her leaving party, came up and squeezed her cheek in fond farewell.

She felt furious but said nothing at the time. This she rationalized by saying she would never have to set eyes on him again, but a couple of years later the incident was still irritating her. This is why I suggested she practised handling it in a different way.

Practice 1

Geraldine is sitting at a table talking to a friend. Frank ambles up and cuts across the conversation to say a fond goodbye, leaning over and squeezing her cheek, and then walks off.

Geraldine is left paralysed with surprise, rage and indignation. She looks at her friend and simply shakes her head in despair.

Geraldine's learning 1

What are the messages in our heads that hold us paralysed and unable to respond?

'I don't believe that really happened.'

'There's no point in saying anything.'

'I'd kill him if I started.'

'It's only because he's had a couple of drinks.'

'I don't want to cause a scene.'

Sometimes keeping quiet leaves us with our personal power intact. Keeping quiet out of fear and powerlessness is not the same at all. This is why it is good practice to get a sense of yourself in role-play (in body and mind), responding to this kind of situation from a position of personal power.

Practice 2

Frank ambles up, squeezes her cheek and walks off.

Geraldine: 'Frank, I...' (*her voice tails off*)

Geraldine's learning 2

It is easy to forget about self-disclosure, which is a pity. Self-disclosure is often the only starting place. Could Geraldine identify her feelings? Anger, indignation and surprise.

Practice 3

Frank ambles up, and squeezes her cheek in a fond farewell.

Geraldine:	'Frank, I feel quite taken aback... I don't like you squeezing my face like that.'
Frank:	'I was just being friendly...'
Geraldine:	'Maybe it was friendly to you, but I don't like it.' She turns her head to carry on the conversation with her friend.

Geraldine's learning 3

Again she found it hard to turn away, to stop, to draw that boundary line. As our anxiety rises, as it does in that situation, we seek to dissipate it by getting into an argument or attempting to placate the other person in some way.

Geraldine was unaccustomed to handling a situation like this and felt it as abrupt, but she felt stronger and somehow clearer. This is what matters. It is the opportunity taken to deal with something as it happens, while it is small enough to handle, instead of giving the impression that we don't really mind, which often encourages more of the same.

While glaring examples of sexual harassment and discrimination are in the minority, less obvious examples of discrimination occur in the form of:

Put-downs by male colleagues

Intimidation by using threatening gestures

Exclusion by men from decision making

Being asked by men to fulfil trivial and demeaning tasks

Being denied credit from male bosses for work achieved

Having a male superior transfer credit to himself

Your expertise and credibility undermined by a male colleague/boss in public

When faced with the reality of these experiences, part of the problem is doubt as to whether they are real or imagined. In the safety of a group setting, naming the experience makes it real. Many women describe these kinds of incidents, most for the first time. Their perceptions can be reinforced and they can learn through these skills to confront these incidents.

Sometimes it is necessary to challenge our perceptions in a group setting as well. This is important. It is easy, when what we experience is denied so habitually, to confuse fact and imagination. All of us confuse the two at times: it is part of living for so long in a world that persuades us that what we see and hear and feel is wrong, inappropriate and irrelevant. Whatever happens, we can become clearer about the other person's behaviour, but more usefully, we can learn how to move from a position of personal powerlessness.

Being stuck in this position keeps us silent. Silence is taken for acceptance; acceptance is translated into permission. Interrupting this cycle is the only effective way to change attitudes. Doing so aggressively conveys a strong message but hostility prevents real listening and learning. Sometimes a humorous response is effective, but humour doesn't always get the message across. Communicating assertively allows a space for exchange, for seeds of real change to be sown.

Viv worked with six male colleagues. She liked them a lot and they worked well together. The problem was the continued banter about the time of the month, being emotional, her hormones and so on. This was often said with humour but it was incessant. Up to now, she had told herself she was being over-sensitive but had withdrawn more and more until she realized that she had got to the point of not being able to be herself any more and being unable to contribute to the team as she wanted to.

Practice 1

This is a classic example of when *not* to wait until it happens again before you tackle it, which is what Viv had imagined doing. Instead, she set the scene, asking everyone to a short meeting at the coffee break.

Six colleagues seated at or near the table, all eyes on Viv.

Viv: 'Look, I've asked you to meet because there is something I want to talk about. It's not easy but you keep putting me down, referring to my hormones and so on…'

A: 'It's only a tease, we don't mean it…'

Viv: 'I know it's a joke but I get fed up with it.'

B: 'We're like that with everyone, you shouldn't take it seriously.'

Viv: 'I know you are… but…' (*losing heart and her way through the dialogue*)

Viv's learning 1

I asked her what was happening and she replied that this was what happened: she would try to make a serious point and it would be dismissed, with humour certainly, but still dismissed.

Practice 2

Viv starts with a stronger self-disclosure.

Viv: 'I've called you to a meeting for five minutes because there's something I want to talk to you all about. When I say something serious, you tend to dismiss it with a flip comment or a remark about my hormones…'

A: 'Playing up now, are they…?' (*getting a smile from the others*)

Viv: 'You're doing it *now* … it makes me really angry.'

B: 'You shouldn't take it so seriously…'

Viv: 'Well, I do take it seriously because I'm fed up with it… (*tears coming to her eyes*)

A: 'You don't have to get upset.'

B: 'You always look as if you can take a joke.'

Viv (*regaining her composure*): 'Look, I haven't said anything before because I didn't want to spoil the "team spirit" and all that. I don't know whether you've noticed but I don't contribute as much as I used to because I don't feel able to be myself … every time I open my mouth to say something, you make some comment about me being a woman…'

(not a joke to be heard, just a slightly uncomfortable silence…)

'… so I wanted to ask you to stop doing it. I'll try to tell you when it happens but you could make an effort to consider what I'm saying before you make a joke.'

Viv (sensing the atmosphere had changed, and moving away from the subject): 'Thanks for meeting. We'd better get back to work. Rob, do you have the number of the lab technician?'

Viv's learning 2

You can lose your way and regain it again while you are talking. Viv learnt the importance of stating her anger clearly instead of blaming and also to ask for a specific change, in this instance, to stop.

twelve

Gender at work – the less visible aspects

In most women's experience at work, visible harassment is far less conspicuous than an intangible feeling of being different, a feeling of alienation. This is both because we are women at *work* and *women* at work. In other words, we can feel alienated from the culture of the workplace and we can also feel different because, as I described before, women at work are a relatively new phenomenon.

It is useful to step back a bit and take an overall sociological perspective of the situation in order to understand our experience more clearly. This helps to understand the background to this sense of being different, of having little affinity with the goals and rules of a contest that feel strange and often conflict with our personal beliefs and values and standards of behaviour.

In any dualistic (either/or) system we have a dominant group and sub-dominant group: one above and one below. Looking at this system, we can see it operating in any political or social structure where this model is the *modus operandi*. If you look at any unequal (oppressed) group historically – native American Indians under the Americans, black South Africans under the white, the Irish under the English, South American Indians under the Spanish, the Aboriginal under the Australians – you see the system in operation.

The vehicle of the dominant group runs on the certainty of its own culture. The word culture here embraces the values, beliefs, principles, attitudes, assumptions and standards of behaviour upheld by the dominant group. This dominant culture stifles the values, beliefs and principles of the sub-dominant group so that the values expressed in the language, tradition, ritual and social behaviour by the dominant group become exclusive. Dominant values become the *only* values. Any values associated with the sub-dominant group become *muted* values.

What happens to the values – traditions, language, ritual and social mores – of the muted group? At best, they go underground, at worst they become extinct. The language is lost: symbols, traditions, music, art, social practices and values are often stamped out forever.

The culture of the dominant group assumes superiority. This assumption of superiority (that the dominant group is inarguably and *naturally* right), is upheld by the muted group as well. The muted group assumes that it is correspondingly and *naturally* inferior. This kind of system needs both assumptions to function. One set of perceptions cannot be maintained without the other: it would be like one hand trying to clap alone.

The conviction that the dominant group is superior leads the muted group to belittle their own goals or values because they do not conform to the 'dominant' goals or values. This means that the goal of the muted group is to aspire *upwards* to be part of the dominant group. It stops challenging the dominant group. Its members learn the relevant rules. They learn the new language and suppress their own. They try to please and fit in to assure themselves of a higher position in the pecking order.

To this end, to both please and survive, the muted group learns strategies of watching, listening, vigilance and alertness. It learns to comply, to second-guess, to go through the motions, to monitor and try always to understand what makes the dominant group tick. This becomes the priority. The dominant group becomes the sole focus: interest in and sympathy with the muted group, the home group, declines proportionally.

The only thing that unlocks this self-perpetuating operation is anger. It will emerge somewhere. At some point, someone will feel understandably angry, as we do when we're oppressed. Anger can emerge as anger: a healthy response to the condition of oppression, an energy for change, an energy to be used for renewal, demolition of superimposed values and reaffirmation of those that have been lost.

More often this anger emerges as aggression which is targeted at the oppressors, ie the ones on top. If aggression rules the day, it is likely that all kinds of punitive actions are carried out in retaliation. These result in an overthrow of the force previously on top, only to establish a different dominant group, thus perpetuating the whole cycle.

It is true that there is no recorded colonization as regards the two genders and yet we can see a similar process in operation. Over the centuries, *one* particular culture, *one* particular set of values, *one* particular way of seeing has been established by certain cultures in the world through overriding and suppressing any alternative.

To understand some of the constituents of this dominant culture, look at the two lists below. These were first introduced to me in Judi Marshall's excellent book *Women Managers – Travellers in a Male World* (John Wiley, 1984) as two different approaches to life:

Rational	Emotional
Analysis	Synthesis
Competition	Cooperation
Mastery	Accommodation
Exclusion	Inclusion
Fixed goal orientation	Awareness of cycles, patterns
Impersonal	Personal
Self-interest	Concern with others
Division	Affiliation

Consider whether you feel more at home with one approach or the other. Many women are comfortable with a certain amount of competition and individualism; they enjoy a structure and flourish within a rational and analytical climate. Many women are less comfortable with an impersonal approach. They prefer to emphasize values of cooperation, teamwork, communication and treating people as whole human beings.

Both these approaches are viable, neither being better nor worse and yet we can easily see that it is the approach described in the left-hand column that tends to dominate.

These particular dominant values and many others retain their hold throughout our culture. The effect of these dominant values reaches into every single aspect of our daily lives: education, sexuality, mental health, medicine, religion, social behaviour. For now we will look at these current values and their alternatives in the context of work.

thirteen

The culture of work

The culture of the workplace is no different from the culture when you leave the office, but it is the workplace that lays particular emphasis on certain goals, assumptions and unwritten rules. Familiarity with the culture persuades us to take it for granted: as with air-conditioning, we become so accustomed to the climate that we forget we are breathing recycled air throughout the entire day.

Uncovering what you perceive as dominant values at work doesn't take long once you give yourself permission to name what you know is there already. What is the less visible structure of interpersonal relations in the workplace: what are the norms of behaviour? What is acceptable or not acceptable? What are the goals? What is prized and what earns disapproval? What do you have to do to fit in? What must you avoid? What does it actually mean to 'act male' or to be one of the boys?

Below is a profile of the dominant culture of a typical organization, assembled from the responses of course participants over the years:

- *Context*. Permanent inequality in a fixed linear direction means that hierarchical power dominates. Those above have more power that those below; they have greater access to various resources and higher remuneration. The higher the position, the more valued the work: directorial/managerial responsibility is given higher kudos than administrative/clerical responsibility.
- *Aims*. The sole goal is financial: the more, the higher the

profit, the better. Ever-increasing profit becomes the only yardstick of success.

■ *Means.* Goals are achieved by competition and battle waged by fair means or foul. Aggression is therefore the sanctioned and primary mode of behaviour. Ruthlessness and bullying are acceptable as the means of eliminating competition.

■ *Climate.* This is impersonal. Individual needs or responses are obliterated by the constant need to uphold procedures. A double standard operates. The traditional power structure and 'the way things are done' will not be much affected by paper policies; this encourages lip-service in response to the need to be politically correct, for example, but without any real (personal) change.

The above profile has three consequences for employees working within this framework:

☐ Integrity is swallowed up by the sanction of dishonesty. This is inevitable and becomes the norm when an individual is judged by performance. How you appear is what matters: you must be seen to be arriving early and leaving late, to be dedicated, to maintain a confident manner at all times. This leads to the well-known phenomenon of bullshitting: appearing always to know what you are talking about, even when in fact you don't.

☐ The blame culture. Following on from the strategy of bullshitting is the necessity to hide, deny or find a fall guy for any error. There is no room for mistakes, for vulnerability, for being human.

☐ The predominance of self-interest. Independent promotion takes precedence over colleagues: you have to watch your back, choose allies, avoid enemies, manipulate people, and fiddle the system.

The prevailing emotion is fear.

These values come as no surprise but it is interesting to see how they dominate. Try to assess your own experience of these values:

Are you comfortable, uncomfortable or resigned?

Do you ever find yourself in conflict with these values?

Are you uncertain of alternatives?

Are there occasions when you blame yourself for not fitting in with them?

Do you ever feel 'unprofessional' precisely because of your dislike of the prevailing norms?

The answer to these questions for many women is 'yes'. Time after time, women (and some men) find themselves working in a climate that they find soul-destroying, frustrating and unpleasant. This climate is not the direct consequence of upholding the actual values or qualities of the dominant approach described in the previous chapter. It is the consequence of the *monopoly* of this approach. In other words, it is a degeneration caused by imbalance, by the dominance of this approach over any clear or equally credible counterpart.

Most women feel alienated in this kind of dominant culture. Part of the difficulty is not having any concrete alternatives. This encourages us to dismiss other options and to be dismissed as woolly, unrealistic, impractical and naive. The combination of a lack of concrete alternative plus the tendency to negate anything that doesn't fit into the dominant culture leaves us feeling powerless, individually and collectively.

Experiences that reinforce a feeling of powerlessness include:

Being discouraged from criticizing or challenging the *status quo*

Confusion and doubt in response to 'double talk', dishonesty and fudging

Incompatibility of values and being undervalued yourself

Not speaking the same language

Lack of confidence

Overwhelming history of tradition if working in an institutional setting

Backlog of emotions to do with the above experiences

Isolation

One step towards regaining some personal power in the situation is to identify and name some alternatives. The next part of the exercise is to discover the underlying values many women sense are *truer* to their own beliefs and preferences. What is important to them? What matters? What do they rate highly? What has meaning? What gives them satisfaction and a feeling of self-respect? What kind of working climate would they prefer?

The picture below represents an alternative based on preferred values identified among a typical sample of course participants:

- *Context.* All levels of work can be valued and can be seen as different and important contributions to the whole.
- *Aims.* As well as the goal of profit, individuals can be important – making room for care of the people/clients/customers who are involved in the work of the organization.
- *Means.* Assertive and open communication has a place at work. People can be consulted and respected, not always told. There is room for integrity, respect and recognizing others' needs.
- *Climate.* This includes personal concern for individuals, for their feelings, needs and responses.

☐ Honesty is important, taking the time to clarify when you don't understand or checking whether someone else understands.

☐ The need for vulnerability and being human, in that mistakes are made. An alternative to denial is to take responsibility for error, to acknowledge weakness and remedy it, to develop one's strengths accordingly.

☐ The importance of seeing self-interest as part of a context related to the whole, and balancing these different needs accordingly. To see others as part of a community, valuing all levels of work and promoting support, harmony and an atmosphere of trust.

The point of doing this exercise is not to compete. The point is to establish a basis of personal power. There is a world of difference between, on the one hand, feeling you are an alien and inadequate because you've got it *wrong*, and on the other, realizing that your personal values are as relevant, important, legitimate as the dominant ones. Your values aren't wrong, just *different*. They are muted values. They are minority values. They are labelled as soft, unrealistic, for the fairies, the birds and cloud cuckoo land. But nevertheless, they are your values and, interestingly enough, shared with many more individuals than you might realize.

Sometimes we do have the external power to enforce muted values. At the end of the first session of filming an assertiveness class for a TV series, I remember seeing a cameraman and interviewer pinning one of the participants against the wall. She had just practised her situation in a role-play and was now being subjected to the 'How exactly did you feel? What did you really want to say?' type of inane questions beloved of TV interviewers when they pounce on someone after an appalling trauma.

I was outraged, of course, because she had become an object to be used for a bit of sensationalism: a permitted and frequent practice in our world, where exploitation is sanctioned according to the dominant values. But for me, she was an individual, vulnerable, in need of privacy and some time to settle herself.

This presented a conflict of values and on this occasion I was able to communicate my values and have them respected for the rest of the filming. This was because I had some external power, in the shape of expertise and a contract which gave me more leverage. Sometimes, in this way we are able to raise awareness of another way of doing things, an alternative structure that allows our values to be incorporated without overriding the practical needs of the others. However, most of the time, we don't have this facility. What can we do when we don't have external power but still feel uncomfortable with the prevailing norm?

Helen found herself in just such a situation with a junior colleague who was to be dismissed because of changes in the company. She didn't like the man particularly but objected strongly to the proposed procedure of waiting until the Friday before he was due two weeks' leave to tell him not to come back after his holiday. She felt strongly that it was unfair to treat him in this way.

She had tried, at the time, to say something to her own superior but had been dismissed as being too sentimental and reminded that this was the way things were done. She was left with a sense of guilt and self-reproach: an emotional state often masking feelings of anger and powerlessness. One constituent of personal power is integrity, being true to oneself. It is loss of this integrity that damages our self-esteem so deeply.

Practice 1

She set the scene by making an appointment to see her superior, giving him due notice of the importance of the matter.

Helen: 'I'm here because I've been thinking about Peter and the decision to sack him.'

Boss   (*shrugging his shoulders*): 'Yes, it's tough but he's got to
         go.'
Helen: 'I feel that he should be told differently… it's not a
         very nice way to do it.'
Boss: 'There's no *nice* way. What do you propose… a collec-
         tion and a bunch of roses?'
Helen: 'No, but I feel that he should be treated decently…'
         (*faltering*).

Helen's learning 1

Self-disclosure is vital here. This means not 'I feel *that*' but an
honest declaration if a value is important to you. If it's important, only you can express this.

Practice 2

Again setting the scene.

Helen: 'This is awkward for me, but why I'm here is because
         I feel angry that Peter should be dismissed in such an
         insensitive way.'
Boss: 'We are not here to be sensitive.'
Helen: 'I realize that I am in the minority, but it's important to
         me. Even if you take no notice, I want to state here
         how strongly I disagree with the manner of Peter's
         dismissal. It has a demoralizing effect on the whole
         department when one person is treated in this
         way.'
Boss   (*looking differently at Helen … does she have a point
         perhaps?*): 'So what do you suggest, a whip round and
         a party?'
Helen: 'No, I'm being serious. He isn't popular, you know
         that. But I would like to see him, with you if necessary,
         and tell him in advance. I think that's fairer to him.'

Helen's learning 2

Recognizing that you are in the minority, of perhaps one, in your particular work setting, but knowing at the same time that what you believe is real, legitimate and relevant is empowering. This is what empowerment – *power within* – is about. It's not about losing face or scoring points. It is less concerned with winning as an outcome than emerging from an interaction with your self-esteem – which relies heavily on being true to yourself – intact.

Powerlessness stems from a sense of inadequacy and inferiority. When your own values are invisible in the main, it is easy to think you're wrong. Speaking up allows you to change your perspective from the perpendicular to seeing in the round.

Helen had no idea whether her superior would alter his position on the matter or whether her preferred approach had as much chance of being implemented as a snowflake surviving in a desert, but by clearly stating her proposed alternative, she felt able to live with herself with more integrity.

You can say nothing. You can speak your mind. You can sometimes enforce your own values. Whatever you do, remember that being different is not the same as being wrong.

fourteen

The value of crazy

For women to effect change and still survive in the workplace and in the world at large, we face a paradox: on the one hand we have to take ourselves seriously. Taking our contribution and authority more seriously includes much of what we have covered so far:

Speaking up

Acknowledging your feelings

Taking responsibility for your opinions and values

Believing your intuition

Valuing your time and effort

Setting limits instead of treading the long and futile path of superwoman, martyrdom and eventual collapse

Acknowledging your anger

Challenging unfair criticism

All this helps to establish a base of person power: serious stuff indeed.

On the other hand, we must learn when to laugh. Laughter and spontaneity are easily overlooked aspects of personal power. There are times when laughter is the best antidote to anxiety.

Becky would arrive for work before 8 am, at least an hour before the others in her department. When she wanted to leave at 5.30, she had a long corridor to walk through past all the open doors of the offices of her bosses who were still at their desks. It was that long corridor walk that she wanted to manage with less stress. It was impossible for her to know whether her fears that others were silently disapproving of her leaving 'early' were realistic or not, but she dreaded her exit every evening.

After a few attempts, we found a spontaneous strategy. Into Becky's mind came the lines of a song of a children's television programme about going home. The comical nature of this appealed to her and she decided to use it. In the next session she reported delightedly that she was now able to walk down the corridor singing this song quietly to herself. She found this an effective and excellent antidote to her paranoia and anxiety, because it made her laugh, even when people looked at her strangely.

Humour certainly has a role to play in all our interactions and, at times, it can help to lighten the atmosphere. Humour plus an assertive approach certainly works well but humour in the form of put-downs, however witty, will always wound.

Another function of laughter is to help us in the midst of entrenched and impossible situations. Dealing with individual incidents is crucial, but individuals are not always the problem. The higher you climb up the hierarchy, the more likely you are to experience a definite but invisible screen of generalized hostility.

This is based in fear of change. Any dominant group struggles to hold on to its power-base because, without it, it ceases to be dominant. This means holding on to control of information, resources, hierarchical position, decision making, policy making, using fair means or foul. The inadmissible fantasy of the dominant group is that the muted group will turn the tables, reverse the positions so that they will in turn become the losers. This is historically what happens and is the lasting hallmark of aggression.

At a more conscious level, it would appear from research in

today's workplace that men are admitting to feeling uncomfortable and even downtrodden in the face of competition from women. Courses are now being offered to help men learn assertiveness training and basic communication skills: how to listen, acknowledge feelings and become more 'human'. Several companies now offer these courses to men both in non-managerial and executive posts.

Unfortunately, even this current trend falls short of any move towards equality. The ethos behind these courses for men appears, significantly, to be based on competition. Women are now seen as having a natural advantage because where an emphasis is on teamwork, it is acknowledged that women possess a greater degree of relational skills than their male colleagues. Instead of imagining that maybe they could learn from women and begin a potentially vital and radical dialogue, it seems that grudging employees now feel disadvantaged in the competition. They are resentful that the newcomers (women) appear to have the upper hand.

This two-fold harassment – resentment at women's presence in the workplace combined with a refusal to reward women for the very qualities that they bring, because of envy – is based on fear of losing status and generates an often unspoken wariness and hostility.

Although women express their frustration with this lack of equality, I am constantly amazed at their general forbearance. Most women suffer all sorts of inequities and still, on the whole, manage to keep going without a felt need to get their own back. This is the base of true personal power.

The key to emotional survival is in knowing when the odds are too highly stacked against you. Making the distinction between what you can change and what you cannot change is essential for health.

What constitutes our personal experience at work is also part of a much bigger pattern in the world. Much of what we experience – a lot of the attitudes, put-downs, criticism and intimidation – is not caused by us *personally*: it is simply that we are representatives of our gender. A younger, 'more attractive' woman will be perceived in one way, an older, 'less attractive' woman will be perceived in another. It is helpful to remember that we are up against a tradition that is immense, historical and collective.

So when you are faced with the impossibility of it all, what do you do? You are, after all, one single individual and there are times when you realize you are up against not only one or two people but a whole system. The system enshrines and upholds all the 'isms' – sexism, racism, heterosexism and so on – and individual attempts to change the system are futile. Frustration and anger fuel energy for a while, but I find that many women fail to distinguish between persistence and useless perseverance.

Aggression encourages us to go on until the opposition is beaten: a long and bloody battle. Assertiveness – which occupies a middle ground, balancing both approaches to life – encourages us to be more creative, to accept our personal limitations and to recognize that to withdraw can be an act of care for oneself. Acknowledging when the odds are too highly stacked against us is not an indication of failure or a cause for humiliation.

Sally was a director of finance in a very large organization, in the minority of one within an all-male department. She had done a few assertiveness courses before and felt able to deal with most situations but she wanted to know how she could have said no when asked by her boss to reorganize the filing system.

The participants had been practising together in small groups and as I came to monitor Sally's group, she was ending a long and arduous role-play. Finally, she practised saying 'No' using the assertive skills, including self-disclosure, in a manner that both she and the rest of her group felt was effective and 'correct'.

Witnessing this, I was struck by the complete incongruity of the situation. We were not just dealing with an ordinary refusal: here was a director of finance being asked frequently by her boss to do menial tasks instead of being given work commensurate with her qualifications and ability. This was not a simple request meriting a simple refusal: this was an example of harassment, a put-down, one person in the dominant position keeping someone else in her (lower) place.

What Sally was dealing with was much bigger than her personal situation, much bigger even than her difficult relationship with this particular man. No wonder at the end of her role-play she looked exhausted and defeated. I sensed that we had to tackle this in a different way because even with the correct assertive skills, she was not communicating from a position of personal power.

I asked her to do one more practice and, this time, asked her not to respond immediately when the request was made, but to wait in silence and see what emerged spontaneously. It is in spontaneity often that we find our own path to personal power. I had no idea what would emerge when she started but I knew that it would be more creative than reciting a formula, however assertive, that was inadequate to the task.

Sally started the role-play again. The request was made. Sally sat in silence. Everyone in the group waited in silence. After a few seconds, Sally started to laugh. It was a deep low belly laugh, slow, then building into a contagious and magical sound, resonating in the belly of every woman in that room. Laughter prompted by the stupidity, the pigheadedness, the arrogance and sheer absurdity of the situation. The laughter was not at any individual, just a profound and healing laugh at the impossibility of it all.

In her laughter, Sally softened, became herself, settled into her own body and stopped tensing for combat in a world in which she had come to believe that combat was her only strategy. This was the point at which she set her limit, at which she felt her own power in the situation and disengaged from a war that would only leave her bloody and bruised at the end. From this place eventually came an unequivocal refusal that was quite disarming in its graciousness. One could imagine that even her boss might be struck by the absurdity of his request, if only for a second.

Over successive meetings, she recommended laughter as an excellent strategy, using it more and more frequently and inspiring others to do likewise. She said that her boss and colleagues would sometimes look utterly baffled and be at a loss for words, but she knew that even if they thought she was 'crazy', she now had a healthy strategy for setting her limits in the face of harassment on such a large scale. She had found a way of coming back to her self: this is true personal empowerment.

The value of crazy does not mean that we don't need to confront individual situations more specifically when this is appropriate, as it often is. The value of crazy applies when we are up against overwhelming odds. It is the value of crazy that enables us to face the impossible, look fear in the eye and survive. Therein lies our power.

fifteen

Women vs. women...

Exploring gender issues at work remains incomplete without looking at the dynamics *between* women at work. What governs our attitude to one another? Course participants often come with questions related specifically to these concerns:

'How do I deal with other women as competitors?'

'How do I cope with women managers who have adopted male-orientated goals and values?'

'How can I communicate with the women at work when there is so much ill-feeling generated by confrontation?'

Obviously, our response to other women will also be based on them as individuals as well as being women. We like or respect some people more than others, regardless of their gender. However, there are less obvious influences affecting working relationships, connected to our shared experience as women (or as men) and if we continue to close our eyes to them, we cannot possibly effect any real change.

One of these is related to the prevailing power structure. Any dominant group regards itself as superior and is also regarded as superior by its corresponding muted group, which, in turn, believes itself to be inferior. This means that women identify with other women as part of an inferior group within a hierarchical structure. This is not usually a conscious identification but one that, nevertheless, exerts a powerful influence over our interaction.

One way this influence emerges is in our mistrust of each other. Most women are wary of coming to a women-only course. In my experience, this is true whatever the content. It takes a lot to trust other women – not because we, as women, are fundamentally untrustworthy, not at all – but because as a muted group in relation to a dominant group, we have become accustomed to comparison and competition.

We measure ourselves; we compare and compete with each other in all sorts of ways, often without being aware of doing so.

Comparison and competition

These are some of the scales we use to assess ourselves in comparison and competition with other women:

☐ *Attractiveness:*
Appearance;
Figure shape;
Skin tone;
Age (and whether it shows);
Hair;
Femininity.
☐ *Intelligence:*
Education;
Status at work;
Experience;
Expertise.
☐ *Social status:*
Accent;
Class;
Marital status;
Number of children.
☐ *Personality:*
Articulacy;

Confidence;
Poise;
Relaxation.
☐   *Wealth:*
Clothes;
Earning power.

Because we are so schooled in measuring power on an up-and-down scale, these differences between us set up an immediate 'ladder', placing those with more power over those with less. This happens in any area of life but, at work, competition is influenced by the scarcity of senior (therefore powerful) positions so it becomes even fiercer, as there are fewer prizes to go around.

We are all susceptible to competition and comparison. Whether or not we actively compete or have taken ourselves mentally out of the running through feeling personally inadequate, insignificant or too unattractive, they remain as twin dominant themes affecting all our interactions.

The dominant/muted structure affects us in another way. We measure ourselves against other women at work because the dominant ethos is 'male' and most work environments, in the higher echelons especially, are governed and dominated by men. This means that the decisions, attitudes, conscious and unconscious values are based in traditional male values.

In this way, we learn to value the 'masculine' over the 'feminine'. We learn to devalue the emotional, intuitive, vulnerable parts in ourselves and in other women and aspire to rational, analytical, strong, impervious qualities. If the latter are strongly developed in us, we value and emphasize them. If not, we often feel unconfident and weak.

One option for women at work is simply to play by the same rules. We can embrace these dominant values, sometimes with a vengeance. This leads to women being described as worse/more aggressive/more competitive/more ruthless than their male counterparts. Women are seen as behaving like men, not only behaving like them, but beating them at their own game.

Although we habitually *de*value our own values, we can still feel betrayed when we see a woman playing these games with the same strategies as 'the boys', aiming for the same goals and achieving them. We sometimes witness the transition at work from one group to the other. It often happens that a woman seems equal while on a parallel rung, but once on a higher one, turns her back on those she has left on the rungs below because she can't afford to be seen to have a vestige of allegiance with them. If she's had to deny and suppress her own values in order to climb, she is unlikely to show any weakness, regret or sympathy with 'alternative' values because this would threaten her newly gained ground: a ground she will unceasingly have to make efforts to retain. This sense of betrayal often makes us far more critical and unforgiving of ruthless or insensitive behaviour in women than we would be of men behaving in a similar fashion.

Even having a more conscious awareness of this dynamic can alter our approach to working with other women. We see our own attitudes, responses and vulnerabilities reflected in those of other women; whether we are compassionate or intolerant of this behaviour will very much depend on how we feel about our own.

Overt and covert competition with each other encourages isolation. This deepens with our individual experience of the difficulties already described in this book, all compounding an inner lack of confidence. Competitiveness undermines our ability to network and give reciprocal support.

One consequence of learning in a group setting is the reduction of emotional isolation, in the process of witnessing so many shared difficulties which cut across the hierarchies of age, experience, qualifications and earning power. More importantly, we witness some of these difficulties being addressed and overcome. The next step is underlining some of our shared strengths.

Towards the end of a course, we look at what aspects of their work give participants the most satisfaction and fulfilment. What promotes a real sense of pleasure and achievement? Below are some typical answers:

- Witnessing a change.
- Humour.
- Communication and being understood.
- Selflessness.
- Living the truth.
- Challenge.
- Creativity.
- 'Open heart surgery'.
- Simplicity.
- Balance.
- Teamwork and a common purpose.
- Professionalism.
- Completion of a task.
- Working hard.
- Being in the moment.

Clearly, some of these reflect the alternative values that we have already described in Chapter 12. They overlap with aspects of internal or personal power. What interests me is that somewhere, deep down, these are the values that underpin the very aspects of work that women find fulfilling. They don't have to be learnt or discovered: simply *un*covered because they exist already.

These values appear to dissolve in the harsher light of the world as it is, with its battles and hassles and dog-eat-dog inevitability. Once aggression is learnt and reinforced every single day of one's life as the norm, these values are eclipsed. And yet they are still there – behind, beneath, on the periphery of our lives, at the edge of our vision, in the back of our minds – never entirely forgotten. Once we can let go of aggression and the need to win, deep down in many of us, we discover these values are still at home: they just haven't been outside to be aired for a while.

What astonishes participants is the *commonality* of values. This, in itself, reinforces the sense of shared values which, in turn, reinforces their right to exist. Even if this realization is only momentary, it helps to diminish the internal experience of isolation and invisibility.

sixteen

... Or bringers of a new order

What do participants gain from these skills? Are any benefits more than short-term?

In the main, participants appreciate the practicality of the skills that they can take back to work with them. Getting someone's attention, giving instructions, setting limits and learning how to stop undermining their personal authority are examples of skills that are extremely useful. The permission to feel, especially to acknowledge feelings of anger, comes as a relief. Another layer of learning involves broader psychological issues: our areas of vulnerability, discovering why we find it hard to set limits, our relationship to anger and to both kinds of power.

Learning these skills should not be underestimated. Often this learning sows a seed of confidence which is enough for a woman to take a leap in her life. Some of the 'leaps' I know of are:

- Anna decided to leave her job, having realized that, despite her perseverance, the hostility she currently faced would not change.
- Pru, having returned to work in her late forties, expanded her horizons and decided to try for a managerial position. She succeeded. The next time I saw her, she had lost weight, restyled her hair and said she'd never looked back.
- Lisa continued to work for an unpleasant woman boss but was more able to set her boundaries, such as putting a stop to tirades instead of passively enduring them and then getting ill.

- The decision to study for an MBA was Ruth's 'leap'. She even asked her boss for time off to do so: something she wouldn't have dreamt of doing beforehand.
- Bridget was able to transform a history of difficult staff relationships. Her manner become less aggressive and she was no longer patronizing when giving criticism. The atmosphere in her department was a lot easier as a result.
- For Hannah, the realization that she'd let herself become swamped by all her roles, leaving her exhausted and depressed, led to concrete decisions: setting limits at work and getting help domestically to look after her elderly mother, even finding time for herself in the form of a weekly massage.
- Mandy was able to initiate a dialogue with a new colleague who'd been offhand and distant. This led to clarifying an unexpected misunderstanding and clearing it so that they enjoyed a much more friendly relationship.
- Christina found the confidence to confront a superior whom she had been trying to pin down for a year to initiate a discussion about her lack of briefing or structure within the department.

An often-voiced benefit of a course is the chance to work together. Having the space in their busy lives to focus on their personal concerns, within a safe and supportive framework, is for the majority of women a real luxury. Working together in this way for three days establishes a different possibility from contact within the normal culture.

First, there is a slow building of trust, which sounds obvious but is often taken for granted. Trust is born of safety. Safety is established by ground rules of confidentiality and a clear working structure. It is also generated by willingness to temporarily set down the competitive battle gear and to be vulnerable.

As this happens, a climate of equality becomes more meaningful: differences are seen as differences instead of better or worse. As the inferior/superior measurement is temporarily suspended, participants begin to see *in the round* instead of along the perpendicular. There is often an expressed wish to continue with this support and sometimes meetings are arranged to try to maintain the collaborative momentum. Networking in this way usually founders as a result of the hidden dynamics already described. In fact, the dynamics are not a problem *per se*: they become problematic because they are rarely addressed in a way that facilitates movement and release from their hold on us.

The other reason it is difficult to maintain momentum is the unchanging power of the organizational status quo. A while ago, a male colleague and I were very keen to offer a course for men and women working *together*: how to cooperate in a new working atmosphere of the future; how to work from a position of cooperation and mutual understanding instead of opposition and mistrust. Four times in two years we offered this course: four times the only subscribers were women. We could only conclude that fear among men was too deeply established, leaving little faith in collaboration.

Over this period, values at work have shifted on paper. The old inflexible hierarchical structure has been shown to be losing effectiveness in terms of productivity and profit. Business gurus encourage rearrangement of company structure along lines that are less perpendicular. This has meant that male managers, accustomed to reporting upwards and having others report to them from below, have found themselves unexpectedly in charge of teams, needing new communication and 'people management' skills.

There are now some smaller and successful companies choosing to operate within a more democratic structure. The decreasing relevance of the old hierarchical system is evident. This could be an ideal moment in time for the (male) gurus who reflect on changing values and structures within the workplace to realize, with appreciation, that women are a great *asset*. Male employees (of all ranks) could learn about different values, about a different meaning of power, about a different approach to people and organizations; they could learn by listening and taking note, by supporting and promoting. But this would take humility and a genuine commitment to equality. In the absence of this commitment, it is easy to interpret the current response as emanating from disadvantaged contenders who are only interested in regaining their previous position of domination and control.

The reason I wanted to write this book was to enable women to challenge the situation in an effective way. Being able to speak up, to challenge, to manage criticism, to handle authority, to set limits are all helped by assertive communication and skills when properly learnt. Above all, I wanted to help transform the disabling lack of confidence.

Being undervalued for the very values that are now coming to the fore is a particularly oppressive trap. Instead of believing that we are competing in a race with inadequate preparation and abilities, the reality is the reverse. We have the skills that are needed because we have not lost touch with the very values of collaboration, personal interaction, emotionality and accommodation that are slowly influencing the way that organizations will run in the future if they are to survive. Precisely because the workplace has been traditionally male-dominated, most men have lost touch with these values, preferring or being entrenched in a culture of competition, impersonal dealings, rationality and conquest.

I am not optimistic about a change from envy to appreciation because fear of change is likely to continue to rule. Only when fear is acknowledged can aggression be diminished. At this point, men could admit they have a lot to learn and consider what equality really implies. But even if, on the outside, aggression and competition continue, my hope is that on the *inside*, women can begin to understand that they are not inadequate or alien, because they are not wrong.

Women are, instead, bringers of a new order, bringers of an emerging model and a different structure. The 'new' values being promoted because they make sense rationally, theoretically and commercially are naturally and spontaneously incorporated into most women's experience. Women do not need to learn these values intellectually: they already exist in their hearts.

Index

abuse 101
accommodation 61, 62
aggression 3, 9, 49, 88, 92,
    93, 110, 121, 122, 138,
    146, 155, 160
  anger and 69–86, 135, 148
  anxiety and 71, 104
  assertiveness and 54,
    111
  interruption as 28
  managing others' 11, 19
  men and 121, 122
  refusal and 51, 53–54
  self-disclosure and 112
alienation 133, 139
anger 4, 5, 11, 66, 142, 157
  aggression and 69–86,
    135, 148
  assertiveness and 80
  expressing 4
  guilt and 142
  managing 5, 11
  setting limits and 66
anxiety 9, 10, 12, 18, 27, 59,
    146
  aggression and 71, 104
  confrontation and 97
  denying 112

managing 5, 14, 29, 33,
    50, 96
  self-disclosure 44–45,
    59
apology 47, 125
assertiveness 2, 3, 6–12, 62,
    119, 140
  aggression 54, 111, 148
  anger and 80
  equality and 24, 75
  handling authority with
    104
  humour and 146
  men and 7, 147
  practising 91
attention 25, 26, 32
attractiveness 124–25, 148
authority 4, 5, 11, 96,
    97–108, 157, 160

being specific 12–14, 78,
    112
blame 45, 46, 47, 66, 69, 71,
    72, 75, 132, 138
boundaries 73, 105, 108,
    125, 129
bullshitting 104, 138
bullying 4, 40, 101, 138

Visit Kogan Page on-line

Comprehensive information on
Kogan Page titles

Features include

- complete catalogue listings,
  including book reviews and
  descriptions

- on-line discounts on a variety
  of titles

- special monthly promotions

- information and discounts on
  NEW titles and BESTSELLING titles

- a secure shopping basket facility
  for on-line ordering

- infoZones, with links and
  information on specific areas of
  interest

PLUS everything you need to know
about KOGAN PAGE

http://www.kogan-page.co.uk